RETHINKING INTERVENTIONS TO COMBAT RACISM

Reena Bhavnani

Commission for Racial Equality *with*
Trentham Books

Trentham Books Limited
Westview House   22883 Quicksilver Drive
734 London Road   Sterling
Oakhill   VA 20166-2012
Stoke on Trent   USA
Staffordshire
England ST4 5NP

© 2001 Commission for Racial Equality

First published 2001

British Library Cataloguing-in-Publication Data
A catalogue record for this book is available from the British Library

ISBN 1 85856 252 X

Designed and typeset by Trentham Print Design Ltd., Chester and printed in Great Britain by Cromwell Press Ltd., Wiltshire.

DEDICATION

This book is dedicated to Stephen Lawrence and his family and friends, and the following people who have died of racially motivated murders – known or suspected – since 1997:

Michael Menson; Ricky Reel; James Tossell; Akofa Hodasi; Remi Surage; Surjit Singh Chokkar; Farhan Mire; Stelios Economou; Harold (aka) McGowan; Joseph Alcendor; Ben Kamanalagi; Jason McGowan; over 60 people injured in bomb attacks in Brixton and Brick Lane; three white people killed in a gay pub in Soho; Liban Ali; Zairean Student; Chinatown 5, New Diamond restaurant; Safaraz Najeib

(*Taken from CARF Bulletin Feb/March 2000*)

Acknowledgements

The research for this book was funded by the Barrow Cadbury Trust.

I would like to thank the Trust, and particularly Dipali Chandra, for providing me the opportunity to carry out this research.

My research assistant, Veena Meetoo deserves a special mention; she worked tirelessly in researching articles and materials for his project and provided me with comprehensive searches as well as summaries of key points. I would also like to thank my Steering Group, Yasmin Alibhai-Brown, Valerie Amos, Phil Cohen, Angela Coyle, Judith Hunt, Gus John, Shushila Patel and Richard Stone for their feedback and helpful suggestions on content.

I would also like to thank Philip Pinto at the Commission for Racial Equality library for his help, and Greville Percival, Research Manager at the CRE for financially supporting this publication.

My editor Kathy Sutton and the Editorial Director of Trentham Books, Gillian Klein have done a marvellous job in making the whole book more readable, because of their unstinting attention to detail. A special thanks goes to my childcare workers, Derya Linal and Maria Szabo, as well as my husband Ian and children Anil and Anjuli for their patience!

Reena Bhavnani

CONTENTS

Author's note

The author recognises that the term *race* is fiercely contested. Writers frequently place quotation marks around the word *race* to indicate that its original use linked it to a scientific biological racism, when in fact *race* is a socially constructed term. To continue to use *race* without quotation marks, it is argued, will have the effect of reproducing it in its original form and legitimate the early meaning of a fixed biological difference. This book has not placed quotation marks around *race* for the following reasons.

Many terms in this book are contested and are associated with different racisms. Examples include: *black, white, racial, ethnic minorities, culture, cultural difference* as well as *race*. This book is about discourse and meanings of words. It is also about the ways these meanings change and are changed through specific relations of power. I am contesting the ways in which words such as *race, racism, culture, identity* and *ethnicity* are used in our society and the ways in which meanings slide and need to be continuously scrutinised. It was not possible to place quotation marks around these and many others so none of these politically contested terms appear in inverted commas. The meanings are explained at length in the book.

1
Introduction

This book arose as a result of the findings of the Stephen
Lawrence Inquiry and, in particular, their emphasis on education and training about racism.

Sir William Macpherson of Cluny began his inquiry in March 1998,
six years after the tragic murder of Stephen Lawrence. The
Lawrence Inquiry was the result of six years of campaigning by his
parents, family and friends. This £3 million inquiry of public
hearings was held over 69 days and consisted of two main parts. The
first examined the causes of Stephen's death and the lessons to be
learnt from it. The second focused on national issues relating to the
investigation and prosecution of racially motivated crimes.

Education and training are central to the inquiry report. Time and
time again, the inquiry condemned the low levels of recognition and
acknowledgement of racism by police at all levels. The failure of the
police training system to tackle colour blindness, ignorance and
denial of racism was heavily criticised. The Stephen Lawrence
Inquiry makes six recommendations (48-54), which address the
central issue of the use of training and education to combat racism.

Many commentators argue that the Stephen Lawrence Inquiry
report, published in February 1999, marked a genuine watershed in
race relations in Britain. Macpherson, a white high-ranking retired
judge, claimed that the Metropolitan Police Force was institutionally
racist. His report made 70 wide-ranging recommendations for
change relating to police accountability, race equality legislation and
for policy reviews on institutional racism across the entire public

sector. After the report was published there were detailed debates in Parliament in March 1999, and the Home Secretary adopted an Action Plan, which set out main areas of work for each of the recommendations. A Progress Report on the Action Plan was published in February 2000.

The success of the Stephen Lawrence campaign by family and friends enabled many others to recall resistance to racial attacks and police responses over many years, not only in the UK but also in Europe. The monitoring groups on racial harassment and the growing number of cases of racial attacks have ensured that racism and resistance to racism remain firmly in the forefront of Britain's agenda.

Aims of this book

The Stephen Lawrence Inquiry Report asked society to rethink racism. This requires that we rethink training to combat racism. It is over twenty years since training to combat racism became widespread in the public sector. There has been hardly any research or evaluation of such training since then. It is now time to take stock. This book is intended to place the Macpherson recommendations in context. It covers three main issues relating to training to combat racism.

❏ The transcripts of the Lawrence Inquiry provide us with the most detailed evidence of public authority and police discourse on racism that the UK has ever had. How far can we use this wealth of information to enhance our understanding of racism and to improve our effectiveness in tackling it?

❏ Over the past twenty years the experience of racism is changing, not only in response to wider political and economic changes but also within both 'black' and 'white' ethnicities in Britain. How far does current training to combat racism take account of the changing nature of racism?

❏ A new political administration has embarked on social policy initiatives designed to promote race equality. It has also adopted wider social policy heavily focused on outputs. Do such initiatives help or hinder effective training to combat racism?

Understanding discourse

The Lawrence transcripts provide a detailed example of police 'race talk'. Discourse making can provide useful clues in how to intervene in the reproduction of such thought and talk between various groups in society. It allows us to focus on the contexts of racism and its expressions.

Racism, however, is not just a matter of bias or prejudice; it is also about the exercise of power and dominance. As Van Dijk observes, racism:

> is not only about biased mental models or prejudiced attitudes or ideologies and their construction or expression in discourse. Racism is about power and dominance, about ethnic and racial inequality, and hence about groups and institutions and more complex social arrangements of contemporary societies (Van Dijk 1999 p.148).

The transcripts provide us with the opportunity to link these two aspects of racism by analysing how thought and talk is reproduced by those in power who lead the discourse, and how such discourse may change in response to wider economic and political changes.

How far has the increasing stress placed on equality, anti-discrimination and human rights affected the discourse on racism amongst various groups and institutions? Has the discourse on racism become coded or invisible in major institutions such as corporate business, parliament, in the media or academia? Does such coding allow overt racism to be expressed elsewhere, giving the impression that racism is characterised by, for example, right wing parties such as the BNP, but not in our own organisations? Does discourse analysis assist us in understanding how racism itself takes on different forms?

The changing nature and forms of racism

Training to combat racism grew out of the early days of the enforcement of the Race Relations Act 1976 and the beginning of the implementation of race equality policies. As the economic and socio-political context has changed, we need to explore how far meanings have changed. We must return to an analysis of key concepts if we are to understand how change has impacted in different ways on different groups. The examination of the changing nature of *different racisms in different contexts* suggests an entirely new approach to raising awareness about racism and challenging it. What, for example, does institutional racism mean? How do young and old people in Britain view their own identities and their own awareness? What is the connection between the changes in economic and political processes and the nature of racism?

The development of social policy

Since the election of a Labour government in 1997 we have witnessed the development of contradictory social policy on race. On the one hand, mainstream social policy is characterised by colour blindness. On the other, since the publication of the Stephen Lawrence Inquiry Report, there has been much central and local government activity, with increased publication of guidance documents on race. In this way race is positioned more as an add-on to social policy. Does such an approach limit its effectiveness?

At the same time, social policy has been dominated by a managerial discourse of targets and quantitative outcomes, as a result of the government's emphasis on public sector accountability. This performance management framework has also been applied to policies relating to race equality. Does such an approach leave room for examining processes, which lead to actual outcomes? If we are serious about the need to challenge racism and promote race equality, we cannot leave such processes undisturbed. If we do, we may be in danger of entrenching or reinforcing institutional discrimination.

Racism awareness and intervention – a new approach

This report concludes that there must be a new approach in education and training on combating racism. One that accepts that racism takes on different forms, operates in different contexts and that organisations may reproduce racism through their own distinct discourse. The old approach of off-the-shelf generic racism awareness training may be a thing of the past, or ought to be.

A new approach is needed, one which:

❑   assists people and organisations to **unravel their own contexts** of racism in relation to the dominant discourse of their organisation

❑   encourages a **long term approach** and fuller examination of cultures inside and outside the organisation

❑   uses **external guidance and verification** methods as a means of developing effective racism interventions

❑   develops a **partnership** approach with external experts to bring about change.

Institutional racism is now on the agenda. We must move forward to drive it out by developing effective forms of intervention. Training to combat racism programmes targeting the police have demonstrably failed. It is entirely possible and highly probable that such failure is endemic in many parts of the public and private sectors. If we are to make the most of the Macpherson watershed, we must ensure that mistakes of old are not repeated. This book indicates tentative first steps forward.

2
Unravelling Racism: Changing conceptions

Education or training will only have transforming effects if they take place in a culture of dominant discourse around challenging racism. If we are to develop effectiveness in challenging racism, we need to understand different racisms and their expressions and dynamism. But this is not enough. We must understand the behaviour and reproduction of everyday racism by individuals and by groups. If we do not understand how racism is produced and reproduced we cannot effectively challenge it.

Racism is multi-faceted and complex in both its specificity and operation. Understanding the nature of racism is crucial to developing effective interventions to challenge it. It has been assumed that institutional racism is the same as racism. This chapter attempts to unravel the concepts of institutional racism and racism and to show that it is unhelpful for them to be used interchangeably. It begins by examining the concept of institutional racism as defined by Macpherson and its relationship to conceptions of racism. There follows an exploration of the changing conceptions of racism, as influenced by the process of globalisation. The nature of new and old racisms are examined in relation to socio-political contexts and definitions of culture, ethnicity and identity are scrutinised. Finally, a focus on new work on everyday racism provides us with new ideas about how to intervene to combat racism with specific target groups.

Defining institutional racism

The Macpherson report defined institutional racism as:

> The collective failure of an organization to provide an appropriate and professional service to people because of their colour, culture, or ethnic origin. It can be seen or detected in processes, attitudes, behaviour which amount to discrimination through unwitting prejudice, ignorance, thoughtlessness and racist stereotyping which disadvantage minority ethnic people (The Stephen Lawrence Inquiry p.28).

This definition encompasses differing conceptions of racism. It incorporates the ideas of black-white racism; of culture and ethnicity; and takes account of racism being 'unwitting'. It appears to be all-encompassing, yet it *excludes* ideas of differing racisms based on gender, class and nation. It reverts to ideas about black/white difference and is associated in our minds with the presence of ethnic minorities – in other words, ethnic minorities as a term is generally used solely with reference to those of South Asian and African Caribbean origin.

Two North American writers and activists in Black Power, Stokely Carmichael and Charles Hamilton, first used the term 'institutional racism' about thirty-five years ago (1967). They made the distinction between individual and institutional racism – the latter being more covert and associated with the respectable institutions of society. Both stressed the historical nature of its origins and the way it was reproduced by *interconnected* relationships across all of society's institutions. They used the concept as a way of understanding the *consequences* of institutional racism rather than to analyse its operation. The term did not denote an ideology, relating...

> rather ... to a range of other processes. These include decisions and policies which had been designed to subordinate/control blacks; active and pervasive anti black attitudes and attitudes which are said to result in racial inequalities (Troyna and Williams 1986 p. 50).

Institutional racism was often used interchangeably with racism, or subsumed under it, giving it a breadth of meaning. In the UK, the term was developed for application here by Humphrey and John (1971), Dummett (1973), Allen (1973) and Fenton (1982) and used to suggest strategies for black activists to overcome racial oppression. But there is still confusion and lack of clarity about the term and it has been subject in its current usage to a number of criticisms.

Firstly, critics point out that it is increasingly being used to refer only to one particular institution where an outcome of inequality, such as black underachievement, is put down to that institution. This is far removed from its original conception, which was to stress the reproduction of racialised inequalities across institutions.

Secondly, critics argue that the concept does not allow for comparisons across class and race or across race and gender, to facilitate understanding of comparative performance of outcomes. This leads to poor conceptual clarity underlying the efforts to change outcomes, particularly since race is seen to be an independent variable separated from other structural inequalities in society. Take as an example GCSE results. It is wholly inadequate to monitor outcomes of disadvantage on the basis of black groups compared with white groups, without taking such factors as class into account. The issues of class, gender and ethnic origin have long been shown to have profound effects on our children's educational outcomes.

Thirdly, because institutional racism is used to analyse policies and procedures, the wider conceptions of racism are not examined. Understanding racism with reference to ideology, nation, identity construction, the role of whiteness and the nature of ethnicity are rendered invisible. Tackling racism comes to be seen as primarily about changing policies and procedures. Racism becomes redefined in social policy, away from its theoretical underpinnings, resulting in confusion in practice and in the design of training courses.

It is therefore important to use the term more precisely. We must analyse it by mapping how it operates through different institutions, the processes that govern particular institutions, and the ways in which individuals and structures may perpetuate these cycles (Troyna and Williams 1986). It may be more appropriate to use institutional discrimination, a term which could then be used to illustrate the *consequences* of racism in particular organisations and across organisations. The terms institutional racism or institutional discrimination should not be used to try to explain the reproduction of racism more generally. If they are, understanding will be limited and interventions only partial. A failure to understand the shifting and complex nature of racism will prevent clarity of objectives in social policy and effectiveness of intervention. So what do we mean by racism today?

Evoking ideas and understandings of racism

When we think about racism from the 1990s to the present, what images do we conjure up? We may think about racial genocide in Serbia or Rwanda. We may remember Rodney King being beaten up in Los Angeles and the ensuing riots. We will recall the murder of Stephen Lawrence. Antisemitic attacks on Jewish cemeteries by right-wing groups may flash through our minds. Our daily newspapers may remind us of one of the many racist attacks against young black men. On further reflection, we may also consider the vitriolic anger against refugees and asylum seekers, or more recently against Eastern Europeans, whipped up in local areas by the media, or the overt attacks against migrant workers in Germany or France. We may conjure up images of exclusion and disadvantage experienced by a variety of groups in the UK, such as the Irish, Muslims and Gypsies. We may see vivid images in our mind's eye of the poor and unemployed in our inner cities.

What we do know is that our notions of racism are changing. We read about ethnic conflicts in the world, which are not based on colour/slavery/colonialism or materialism alone. We read about the differences in labour market participation and material success of different ethnic minorities (Modood 1997); we have recently seen information from the Office for National Statistics about Bangladeshi girls outperforming white girls in GCSEs; we read about young black people defining themselves as British Indian, say, or see the fusion of different cultural forms in music and on television (such as Asian Dub Foundation; Goodness Gracious Me).

At the same time, however, we know that certain things are not changing. We continue to see a rise in racist attacks in the UK and Europe based on colour. We continue to hear about the exclusion of African Caribbean and South Asian origin women and men from senior positions in employment (Davidson 1997). The pay gap between the majority of black women and white women, black men and white men (Bhavnani 1998) persists.

We live in both new times and old times. Institutional and structural racism sits side by side with the increasing culturalisation of ethnic communities of colour. On the one hand, there is discrimination faced by poor black people, for example, in housing and education. Although this discrimination may be an expected consequence of institutional racism, the ways this operates for differing groups will need further differentiation, so that appropriate social policy interventions can be devised. On the other hand, complex issues between and within black groups have been raised by the Salaman Rushdie affair (Anthias and Yuval-Davis 1992) or the incorporation by the young black and white generations, of new multicultural identities (Cohen 1999). These old and new racisms may be connected, and not as separate as they at first appear. Certain common patterns of racism continue to reproduce trends in racist practices and ideologies. It has also been argued, however, that these racisms are differently located and in a constant state of flux. Recent academic literature has stressed the changing nature of ethnicity and identities (Hall 1996; Mac and Ghaill 1999), including notions of diasporic identities for all (Gilroy 1994; Brah 1998).

Globalisation and changing conceptions of racism

In the few hundred years up till the middle of the twentieth century, the advance of slavery and colonialism was dominated by the concept of race as a biological fact. Racial categorisations based on scientific racism have gone hand in hand with economic exploitation, such as slavery or indentured labour. Segregation policies in South Africa and North America and the colour bar in the UK were clearly influenced by the thinking of the Social Darwinists, who emphasised racial hierarchies and classification as god-given. Supposed biological inferiority was used to justify overt segregation or explicit exclusion. This gave rise to a focus on phenotypical features such as skin colour, although in many parts of Europe people preferred to speak of xenophobia or hostility to foreigners (Castles 1996).

In the 1960s and 1970s successful anti-colonial struggles combined with the growing Civil Rights movements and the introduction of legislation covering human rights and equality became part of most countries' agendas. This was the era where integration was possible and efforts were made to encompass cultural difference. This era created the 'new racism' (Barker 1981) and the 'culturalisation of racism' (Essed 1991).

Ideas of cultural differences and ethnicity became closely associated with the idea of race. These were linked to the new discourses of tolerance. The UN and other international bodies laid down a range of conventions and resolutions concerning racism. These moved from the biological notion of race to the idea of race as social construction (Castles 1996).

New social policy initiatives and anti-discrimination legislation based on equality and multiculturalism were introduced in North America and the UK. The new legislation was accompanied by a shift away from assimilation policies into the host society and to-wards cultural pluralism. Concepts of discrimination and equality were indelibly linked with the idea of culture and ethnicity.

Globalisation and social change

These shifts in the conceptions of racism are linked also to the pro-cess of globalisation. The last quarter century has been marked by transformative technological, economic and political change. Material and social relations have shifted. The technological revolu-tion, the liberalisation of world trade and the financial markets has led to a growing interdependence of nations. Technological change has accelerated the process of global communications. The restruc-turing of capitalism and the global movement of capital and labour have further increased the interdependence of nations. Thus culture, nation and identity are and continue to be caught up with concep-tions of racism. These changes have interacted with the racisms of globalisation.

The impact of globalisation and changing nation states has forced renewed thinking about the conceptions of racism, the notions of ethnicity and culture and the axis of white versus black in relation to racism. This has led to new research paradigms of how racism is produced and reproduced in everyday life. The examination of everyday racism, either through language in the media, government or academia, or in other cultural forms such as music, film, television and advertising has blossomed.

Many writers have alluded to the uncertainty created by global change and the resulting 'crisis' of identities (see for example Castells 1996: Volumes 1-III). For example, the fragmentation of the Soviet Empire, the unification of Germany, the mass movement of migrant labour and the restructuring of the labour markets with women at their centre have all led to new thinking about ethnic, gendered and national identities. These identities change as time passes and new identities are (re)-created and (re)-imagined. Old imaginings of nation related to ideas of a unified race or ethnicity are shifting and new ones are being created and fought over. There are growing inter-nation/intra-nation conflicts based on ethnicity.

Most writers examining these changes argue that racism shifts and differs with regard to different contexts. It affects different groups and areas/locations differently. (Gilroy 1987; Anthias and Yuval Davis 1992; Hall 1992a; Hall 1992b; Mac an Ghail 1999). Globalisation creates new racisms in much the same way as it creates a multiplicity of capitalisms, with countries and regions increasingly differentiated in the way they adapt to international market-led processes. No longer should we talk about one racism but about multiple racisms, as Gilory argues when discussing the conception of race formation:

> The concept supports the notion that racial meanings can change, be struggled over. Rather than talking about racism in the singular, analysts should be talking about racisms in the plural. These are not just different over time, but may vary within the same social formation or historical conjuncture (Gilroy 1987 p.38).

The context of globalisation has focused analysis on different racisms concerning the following themes: nation; ethnicity and culture; black/white racism. While these may be linked, they may need different interventions and may require appropriate awareness raising. All these themes are integral to developing effective social policy and raising awareness about racism.

Racism and nation

The idea of nation is socially constructed. It changes in relation to economic, social and political processes. Nation is an 'imagined community', imagined *'because the members of even the smallest nations will never know most of their fellow members, meet them, or even hear them, yet in the minds of each lives the image of their communion'* (Anderson 1983 p.38 quoted in Cockburn: 1998 p.6).

Nations are reconstructed also on the basis of gender and race. Constructions of nationhood involve specific notions of manhood and womanhood. Britannia is, for example, evoked in nationalist discourse, but she is, like other women, not autonomous, but linked to the patriarchal structure of the family. As the family is seen as a microcosm of the nation, women can guarantee the bloodline and so-called 'purity' of the nation. (Cockburn 1998; Yuval Davis 1997). They may even be the carriers of cultural traditions.

The concept of Great Britain really came into being in the last three hundred years (Runnymede Trust 2000). This concept had to be evoked and imagined so that it could mean something for all those who lived within its borders. The secularism of public life helped people to imagine a more homogeneous society by means of images and metaphors alluded to by various writers:

> Shakespeare's sceptred isle; 'this other Eden, semi-paradise'; Stanley Baldwin's sights and sounds of the countryside ('the tinkle of the hammer on the anvil smithy, the corncrake on a dewy morning ... the sight of a plough team coming over the brow of a hill'); John Major's warm beer and elderly ladies cycling to communion through the early morning village mist; ... all these examples make it clear that image, metaphor and shared symbols play a crucial role in constructing and maintaining the idea of England as an imagined community. They not only express solidarity but also construct a solidarity that was not there before (Runnymede Trust 2000 p.20).

The notion of Britishness has a long and imagined history, interpreted by differing communities through location, region, class, gender and ethnicity. As Hall points out, Britishness has never been a oneness. It has been contested throughout history, whether through establishing the primacy of Parliament, the right for the poor and for women to vote, tackling child poverty, the right to trial by jury or the creation of the National Health Service. All these advances have been fiercely contested and have had differentiated groups throughout British society supporting, opposing, compromising (Runnymede Trust 2000). The national identities of Scottishness, Welshness and Irishness all have a conflictual past with England and with certain sections of England.

The social pluralism/differentiation of British society continues rapidly. A key change in the late twentieth century was the mass movement of people entering a huge number of nation states, so compelling a more overt multiculturalism and diversity (Runnymede Trust 2000). The UK has experienced immigration not only from its own ex-colonies but also more recently from countries such as Iran, Ethiopia, Bosnia and Kosova. People fleeing wars, political regimes and famine have sought refuge in other nation states. In the UK, we are seeing new peoples becoming (or not?) part of nations, either as economic migrants or as positively recruited from abroad to fill skilled positions in the UK, as nurses, teachers, doctors, social workers and, recently, IT specialists (*The Economist* May 6th 2000).

Over the past twenty years there have been many attempts to re-define and contest Britishness. The loss of Empire, the distortion of ideas of the East and West, a growing integration with a European identity and a forced multi-cultural society has led to a series of contests on the definition of finding what Englishness or Britishness means. Nationhood in Britain has repeatedly excluded black people.

This exclusion of black people from being British or from full citizenship has important implications for the very idea of race and racism. It is based on colour. These unspoken racialised connotations are brought more to the fore when outsiders are spoken about in the dominant discourse. The history of immigration and nationality legislation has been based on excluding those peoples from Britain's ex-colonies who were defined by their colour. The 1968 and 1971 Acts strengthened institutional racism in immigration control; the 1981 Nationality Act established citizenship to be based on patriality, i.e. those whose parents or grandparents had been born in Britain. The 1988 Immigration Act made residents in

15

Britain prove they could maintain their relatives here without recourse to public funds, thus implying that black people were a burden on the Welfare State. Harmonisation of stricter immigration and asylum controls in Europe led to the 1993 Asylum and Immigration Appeals Act, with visitors losing the right of appeal against entry (Bhavnani 1994).

Black people were repeatedly seen as unwelcome, as not part of Britain; it was agreed that restrictions on their entry would lead to better social or race relations. This argument was first used in 1905 about Jews fleeing Eastern Europe. These days exclusion continues to apply to asylum seekers (see Chapter 4). Although many recent asylum seekers are white and come from eastern Europe, the vitriol has turned particularly on the Romany gypsies, characterising them as 'beggars', thus transporting the racism they faced in their own countries of origin to this country. The Home Secretary has been unwilling to believe their lives were under threat through racism, despite evidence to the contrary (*The Observer* 2 July 2000). Recently the demand for a bond from those arriving from the Indian subcontinent made more explicit the relationship of immigration from the ex-colonies with colour.

It is claimed that there is a crisis of British identity in the light of devolution, a forced multiculturalism, the privatisation of British institutions and the pressure to became part of Europe. This panic about refugees and asylum seekers is a crisis about British identity. This focus on what is British and the ideas of belonging and citizenship remain central to awareness about racism and helps to racialise and exclude people who are entering Britain for the first time. Historically, the discourse about the relationship of immigration to bettering race relations has been a theme in British politics for most of the twentieth century. The association of racism with colour pervades current arguments.

Racism, ethnicity and culture

According to Raymond Williams (1976), culture is one of four or five key concepts in modern social knowledge. It evokes several meanings. He takes us through the origins of culture as being initially associated with agri-culture. What began as the tending of crops and animals became associated with the processes of human development (du Gay 1997) and the word became associated with 'way of life'. Within the human and social sciences it has a wider meaning:

> Williams calls this the social definition of culture, 'in which culture is a description of a particular way of life which expresses certain meanings and values implicit and explicit not only in art and learning but also in institutions and ordinary behaviour. The analysis of culture from such a definition is the clarification of meanings and values implicit and explicit in particular ways of life, a particular 'culture'. (Williams 1961 p.57 quoted by du Gay 1997 p.12)

Williams placed culture as central to meaning, communication and language. This approach led to the growth of what is now termed cultural studies. Reflection about modernity, post-modernity, and post-colonialism has had a wide impact on the nature of social sciences. Within the discipline of sociology, teaching and writing about social structures and class as the framework of sociology has been questioned. The emphasis on material reality and social structures had relegated analysis of culture to an inferior role; there was no empirical method in which one could verify these kinds of analyses. Culture was after all based on non-tangible signs, symbols, images, languages and beliefs (du Gay *et al* 1994). But recent years have seen an upsurge of what one author calls 'the turn to culture' (Barrett 1991). A turn to culture and the ways in which cultures are reproduced and produced together with the politics of identity have acquired increasing importance in our interdependent world.

The impact of new technologies and immediate access to changing lifestyles and cultural exchanges across and within localities, nations and continents stimulates experimentation with new cultural forms and identities. The analysis of literature, film and television, for example, has given rise to much writing about how race is conceptualised in imagery and how representations of race frequently alter. These studies add weight to the *'presumption of single monolithic racism ... being displaced by a mapping of the multifarious historical formulations of racisms* (Goldberg 1990: xiii' quoted in Solomos and Back 1996:18).

17

'Ethnicity' has often been used interchangeably with 'race'. The use of the term dates from the 1930s. It was first used by American sociologists studying European immigrant groups and their relationship to US society. These sociologists used ethnicity to describe people who perceived a shared identity on the basis of culture, descent and territory (Morgan 1985). Ethnicity is essentially a process of group identification.

The analysis of ethnicity in Britain normally begins with a study of the immigrants from the New Commonwealth in the 1950s. Yet we are all members of an ethnic group, whatever our colour (Bhavnani 1994). To use ethnicity to discuss the location of black groups only as in 'ethnic minority communties' is erroneous. We end up using phenotypical features (old racism?) and associate skin colour with ethnicity:

> For example, ethnic monitoring is carried out on the basis of skin colour – to the detriment of valid data collection and ethnically sensitive service provision sometimes assumes needs on the basis of appearance – to the bewilderment of recipients. (Macey 1995 p.131)

Also problematic in the marking out of ethnic groups as separated by culture, is an assumption of homogeneity within the group itself. We know that the heterogeneity of groups categorised as having one culture is absurd. Firstly, differences in culture may be separated by origin and 'routes' but a variety of black groups interact with and influence as well as being influenced by so-called mainstream society (Runnymede Trust 2000). They are constantly forming new social mixes and creating new cultural forms and identities. For example, not all Muslims interpret their religion in the same way; there are wide differences between Indians in the type of work they do and their involvement in mainstream institutions; there are increasing separations between younger Bangladeshis and their family traditions. In addition, men and women within many of the different groups are represented differently.

Differences within ethnic groups are also dynamic, interacting with the structures of society, influenced by and influencing each other. All too often these differences are rendered invisible in strategies to counter racism. Failure to recognise differences within ethnic groups

and their changing nature subscribes to a 'narrow ' and fixed definition of culture (Phoenix 1988) and reinforces cultural racism:

> We need to be theoretically and politically clear that no single culture
> is hermetically sealed off from others. There can be no neat and tidy
> separation of racial groups in this country. It is time to dispute those
> positions which, when taken to their conclusion say: 'there is no possi-
> bility of shared history and no human empathy'..... Culture even the
> culture which defines the groups we know as races, is never fixed,
> finished or final. It is fluid; it is actively and continually made and re-
> made. (*Gilroy* 1992 quoted in Macey 1995 p.131)

The cultural differences *within* communities are also marked by
overarching material differences. For example, there are differences
between those who live in the poorer inner cities and these in
affluent suburbs; there is a growing polarisation between Indian
groups, some of whom are extremely rich, some exceedingly poor;
the differences of educational achievement between African Caribbean origin boys and girls; the higher educational achievements of
young men and women of Chinese origin relative to white young
women. These material differences are part of a view of culture that
is dynamic and integral to the shaping of people's beliefs, practices
and identities. Within any cultural group, there are variations according to age, class, gender and sexuality.

Black/white dualism

This heterogeneity within identified groups across age, generation,
religion, education and labour market achievements suggests we
need a different approach to the old ways in which racism and antiracism are conceptualised. The dominant view in the 1980s was the
opposition between black and white as the defining mark of racism
and its mirror image of antiracism. As we have seen, this black/white
dualism has also been used in defining and implementing policies
against institutional racism. It has also influenced much, if not most
of, the public policy and training on race issues (see Chapter 5).

The heterogeneity of blackness has been unpacked little by little but
unpacking whiteness is a relatively new development. Much writing
on the need to focus on whiteness has emerged from the United
States (for example see Lipsitz 1998; Hill 1997; Delgado and

Stefancic 1997; hooks 1989). There have also been some studies in the UK (Cohen 1997; Phoenix 1997; Frankenberg 1997; Back 1996; Hewitt 1986). Most argue that whiteness as a category has to be distinguished from the term white used in relation to white supremacy. This distinction allows people to understand how whiteness functions without having to label anyone a racist (Wander, Martin and Nakayama, 1999).

Key points emerging from the unpacking of whiteness include:

- White is seen as the majority, the norm, giving the concept status, which implies that it is tied to power

- Whiteness lacks racial/ethnic features, thus making it invisible

- Whiteness becomes naturalised so that it means nothing except a category which excludes any cultural traits. Such traits are applied only to minority groups

- Whiteness is confused with nationality, which is an expression of power in that it relegates members of black ethnic groups to a marginal role in national life

- White people who refuse to label themselves as white are asserting that ethnicity can only be applied to non-whites. Thus white does not seem like a label (Nakayama and Krizek 1999).

It has been argued there is a pressing need to deconstruct whiteness in relation not just to racialisation but also to identity formation (Brah 1992).

Identity

The question of cultural identity or identity crisis as affected by global transformations has been studied at length and is part of common discourse. Previous debate on identity had been confined primarily to psychology. Here there was an implication that identities were singular, fixed and perhaps related to a core of self (Woodward 1997). Recent writing has questioned a fixed notion of identity and suggested that we all make and remake multiple identities and that these shift and change in differing contexts.

The issue of cultural identity aiming to achieving a oneness or cultural belongingness underlying all other superficial differences (Hall 1997 p.4) can be challenged. In reality, all identities are fragmented, never unified, often intersecting and multiply constructed. Someone can, for example, be Indian, English, a woman, a mother, a migrant and a jazz musician and so on all at the same time and these identities change as contexts change. They may even conflict with one another; such as Indian/English, mother/worker. Thus education and intervention is misconceived when it is based upon the concept of a single identity formed through ethnicity.

We can only experience our sense of self socially. Identification with someone else takes place through the representation of images, ideas and thoughts via language, or via other media of communication. These identifications give meaning to our experience. Identification suggests a common origin or shared characteristics with another person or group or with an ideal. It has been argued that such identification is based from the start on ambivalence. For one's first identification normally begins with one's parents who are at the same time both love objects and objects of rivalry. This ambivalence is grounded in fantasy, projection and idealisation. It is part of our unconscious, which has been repressed and is expressed through dreams or what are called Freudian slips. The unconscious follows its own system of thought and is structured like a language. The ambivalence so produced is based on splitting different parts of ourselves into masculine, feminine, good, bad etc. (Hall 1997; Rattansi 1994). We can only form our identities through representations of those who may be like ourselves, via language, images, film, and art. These identities position us as to who we are, but this *who we are* is always looking for the 'ideal', the perfect fit (Hall 1997). It is never final, never complete.

Unconscious unmet desires are therefore powerful and produce ambivalence around white, black or other identities. Fanon (1986) argued that the black man experienced himself negatively 'through not being white', a powerful combination of the psyche and the social. Through the history of slavery and colonialism, the black man and woman were constructed as sexual, whereas whites were not.

Black people were attributed with characteristics of emotion, magic, primitiveness, all of which the white man did not at the time need.

Rational arguments are too simple a way of challenging racism, since these opinions and views are part of the unconscious, and if they have not been expressed, they are not amenable to rational discourse. The role of the unconscious in racism discourse is powerful. Cohen has argued that it is an important tool to use in education (*CARF Bulletin* 1997 p. 8-9). He considers the racism of white working class young men to be intrinsically tied up with identity and their body image, and that educators have to construct new identities with them as partners and learners, so that contradictions around racism can be resolved. Cohen argues that if the only or key strategy is to censor racism it will generate resistance, particularly in the context of school disciplinary cultures.

Understanding and challenging racism through the unconscious requires a longer term educational approach. Attitude change is a complex issue that is not amenable to the giving of facts or persuasion by statistics. This complexity also suggests that short term training courses based on a rational approach will have minimal effect – or worse, merely repress racism.

Everyday racism

Attention to everyday expressions of racism, ethnicity, identity has been incorporated into the theoretical map by Essed (1991). She argues that the current concepts of institutional and individual racism, and the relationship between them, are problematic.

She maintains that these concepts sever the individual from the institution, as if this individual racism is a '*qualitatively different racism, rather than different positions and relations through which racism operates.*' (Essed 1991 p.36). She further argues that institutional racism has been used in various studies to narrow the problem down to institutional discrimination. Since these approaches to discrimination are pragmatic, they are oriented towards changing policies, practices, procedures, setting targets, and take insufficient account of ideology in structuring and producing racism. She suggests that racism is created and recreated through routine practices by 'agents', by human beings. For Essed, racism is an ideology, a structure but also a process, because *'structures and ideologies do not exist outside the everyday practices through which they are created and confirmed'* (p.44).

She goes on to locate the processes of everyday racism as:

> the integration of racism into everyday practices ... that activate underlying power relations. This process must be seen as a continuum through which the integration of racism into everyday practices becomes part of the expected, of the unquestionable, and of what is seen as normal by the dominant group. (Essed 1991)

Furthermore, Essed stresses that everyday racism implies that people are differently involved according to their gender, class and status. Such racism operates through direct interaction and indirect interaction via the press or other media, or via government discourse and other indirect forms. The more access human agents have to power, the greater the consequences for racist practices.

This attention to everyday racism is not included in the definition of institutional racism as currently understood. Sir William Macpherson put the blame for racism on culture and processes. 'Don't blame individuals, blame the organisation' is a reasonable interpretation of his analysis. On the other hand, Sir Paul Condon felt blame should be attached to individuals but not to the organisation as a whole (see Chapter 6). Such opposing views appear irreconcilable.

Conceptions of racism, identity, ethnicity, culture, nation

Some conclusions:

- We can no longer accept a black/white dichotomy of the operation of racism.

- The heterogeneity of communities, black and white, cuts across class, gender, sexuality, ethnicity, age and disability.

- Racism is historically specific – i.e. the specificity of how racialisation takes place in particular contexts needs to be understood.

23

- Racism is not one thing – it changes with contexts. This makes it difficult to teach about in a singular, homogeneous or simple way.

- Human agents reproduce racism in everyday situations. People have a range of identities, all of which they identify with at particular instances of time and place. Some identities, such as 'being' white, are often invisible and not openly discussed. These identities are part of how racism is experienced, expressed and interpreted.

- Racism is conflicting and ambivalent – people's identifications, anchored in both the conscious and the unconscious, are grounded in projection, fantasy and idealisation. It is about the 'other' as part of you e.g. BNP activists having black friends. It is not simply a matter of us *against* them.

- Cultural racism does not always refer to colour directly but implies inferiority through the ways in which different groups are seen to live. The idea of colour blindness is part of the development of cultural racism. Colour blindness is challenged when overt and covert racism based on phenotypical features is revealed, such as the exposure of the racist murder and the institutional racism in the police force found in the Stephen Lawrence Inquiry.

- The racisms concerned with culture, class, gender and nation are developed and reproduced differently, although there may be certain prevailing overall patterns.

These differing manifestations of racism suggest its multi-faceted and complex nature. Racism cannot be viewed in the light of one explanation or one theoretical framework. There are macro racisms and micro racisms. These different racisms need to be examined in their specific contexts. We go on to do this in the next chapter.

3
Unravelling Racism:
the specificities of racism

There is a need to move beyond a conceptual framework,which begins with making minorities the object of inquiry. (Mac an Ghaill 1997 p.145)

It is important to study the ways that ideas about race and racial difference move between private and public realms of everyday life: the home itself, the street, the school playground, the clinic, the hospital, the church, the supermarket and other places of congregation. (Ware 1997)

Introduction

As we have seen, the conceptions of racism are constantly changing in response to specific historical and political conditions. Over the last twenty years racism in dominant discourse has moved from scientific biological arguments towards cultural racism. The notion of cultural differences and a multicultural approach to social policy masks racism (Wimmer 1997). In fact, such discourse provides a breeding ground for both far right and everyday racisms. Because the essence of multiculturalism lies in the idea that every culture is worth protection, so multiculturalism can be re-interpreted as a right of the indigenous to defend their homeland against 'mixture' (Wimmer 1997; Solomos and Back 1996). Cultural difference becomes a way of assigning blame for exclusion and poverty.

This period of history is marked by, on the one hand, the resurgence of old racism, based on black/white duality, and, on the other, the development of new racisms based on cultural differences. Increasing global interdependence threatens the nation state. It enables racism to be more overtly linked to the ideas of sovereignty and nationhood. At the same time the definition of blackness as a political identity has fragmented as a result of the resurgence of 'ethnicism' and increased cultural differentiation (Solomos and Back 1996). Changing multiple identities are based on both the unconscious and the conscious.

This chapter is concerned with unpacking the contexts of racism and their specificities. How different racisms are overtly expressed but also coded must also be considered when unravelling racisms. For different racisms reveal a bigger and broader picture of the reproduction of racism. A greater understanding of these complexities will lead to more effective strategic interventions.

The chapter draws attention to existing research which shows that racism is not a homogeneous phenomenon. It looks at how dominant discourse can disguise and conceal other racisms. It shows how there are wide variations, contradictions and ambivalences around racism and its expressions. It also explores evidence of initiatives that have attempted to address the specificities of racism. It shows how some racisms are more visible than others and how dominant discourse can create the idea that only one type of racism exists. This essentialism can mask other more powerful racisms which may legitimate less powerful ones. Occupational culture, for example, can have a profound effect on the creation and reproduction of racism in particular groups.

Black as homogeneous

The issue of blackness has provoked much research and writing. Black perspectives in social work issues argue that there is a singular view of what it is like to be black. Social policy workers often argue about having black consultation mechanisms, or about running courses for black young men to reinforce a positive black identity, for example, in the Criminal Justice system. Such views have been criticised for promoting a singular view of what it means to be black. They assume people have a need to have one identity and totally ignore the multiple nature of identity formation.

Ethnicity, region and family location profoundly affect how different groups and individuals see themselves and are seen. The constructions of women and men of differing ethnic origins has its roots in slavery and colonialism (Centre for Contemporary Cultural Studies 1982; Hall 1997; Stoler 1997), but are maintained and reproduced specifically in differing contexts, such that age, gender and class interact to produce different black racisms. For example, constructions of African Caribbean origin women are different from those of Indian origin women or women of Bangladeshi origin. Ideologies of black Caribbean origin women have been constructed through their position as domestics and surrogate mothers to white families, rather than in relation to their own families (Carby 1982). Employers do not see these women as either leaders or managers. Research shows that Asian origin women employed in the financial sector are less likely to be employed on the customer service side. This is partly related to employers' perceptions of their language and communications skills (Gray *et al* 1993).

In the context of the changing labour market, these racialised constructions continue, but in changed forms. Recent research in Coventry found that employers frequently hold negative stereotypes of Asian women but, also, that ostensibly positive stereotypes could equally be disadvantageous. Employers reported that changes in the nature of work were leading them increasingly to seek employees who were flexible, able to exercise their initiative and ready to carry responsibility for checking their own work and acquiring new skills. They were frequently ready to characterise Asian women workers as loyal, hardworking and uncomplaining. But these supposedly 'positive' stereotypes were not often perceived to be compatible with the new requirements and demands of the modern work place (Gray et al 1993).

There may be differences not only within 'black' but also between black groups themselves. For example, racial name-calling and abuse takes place between all ethnic groups, Celtic, African Caribbean, white English, Indian, Pakistani and so on. There are tensions within groups on gendered and generation lines in relation to marriage. There are conflicts between South Asian origin religious groups. Recent project work with youth has attempted to resolve such conflicts with good effect (Slough Borough Council *Ekh Saath* 1998).

White racisms and the focus on young working class men

In recent years the racism among young working class men has received a great deal of media and government attention. Recent figures from the Home Office show that racial crime offenders are primarily young and primarily men. According to the Home Office, racial incidents rose sharply from 13,878 in 1997/98 to 23,049 in 1998/99. Some of this rise may be attributable to improved recording practices. However, what is clear is that there is a preponderance of young men among the perpetrators. There is an assumption about their class background; we have little information about the socio-economic status of either perpetrators or victims. We know that nine out of ten perpetrators are white. More than half of all racially motivated offences are carried out by those under the age of 24 (CRE 1999). Young men aged between 16 and 25 carried out 61% of attacks against Asians. Young men aged 16-25 carried out 40% of attacks against people of African Caribbean origin. There are high offending rates amongst teenagers of racially motivated property damage (CRE 1999).

Whilst these figures show that there may be some reason to focus on this section of the population, the fact that they have received most attention may be because their racism is overt and thus amenable to media coverage.

Media coverage has tended to focus on 'racist thugs' and 'football hooligans'. Such coverage may not be useful. Why should everyone who lives on an estate be labelled racist by newspapers (Hewitt 1996) or all football supporters be called young racist thugs (*The Guardian*, 4 July 2000)? The Macdonald Inquiry into the murder of Ahmed Ullah and racial violence in Manchester schools (1989) showed the clear differences between young people in their expressions of racism and in their willingness to challenge it. The Inquiry revealed that these differences are not easily attributable to categories such as black/white or men/women.

28

Even among those who express overt racism there are differences. Willems argues that to focus only on violent youth is misleading. Violent youth represents only a minority of youth who may potentially have racist attitudes (1995). Theories of youth violence often assert that social tension is linked to disintegration and breakdown of communities. But this violence usually occurs in highly integrated societies, which have strong links to ethnic group and kin and that these ethnic groups and kin may be tightly integrated. Groups of anti-foreigner activists are too heterogeneous to be labelled as racists or right-wing extremists.

Willems used opinion polls, police records and news reports to determine the distribution of xenophobic attitudes amongst young men. He argues that the fact that there has been an increase in the willingness to participate in violence does not necessarily mean that there are *more* racists. We have to look at what encourages the violence. It is possible that these young men might

- be involved in far right politics

- be ethnocentric and hostile towards foreigners but not involved in far right politics

- have a propensity towards violence and not be involved in far right politics with no political goal

- be fellow travellers and identify with any right-wing extremism, but not be hostile towards foreigners. These people are usually from a middle class background with no 'serious' background problems. For them, group solidarity is important and pressure to conform is at the forefront.

In exploring 'white' racisms it becomes apparent that particular groups are generally absent from the debate. Researchers rarely, if ever, comment upon their racist behaviour or the racism in their discourse. For example, there is virtually no research on how white women across different backgrounds speak about racism and their whiteness. One of the first studies in this area appeared in a book called *White Women, Race Matters* (Frankenberg 1994). She interviewed thirty women in the USA of diverse class, age and marital status. Her work revealed a variety of expressions of racism amongst women. These were related to dominant discourse and shifting historical moments in racism: colour blindness; clear dividing lines between racists and non-racists; a belief that affirmative action discriminated against white people; acknowledgement that equality was here to stay; the willingness to discuss difference with reference to ethnic groups in other countries, as opposed to hesitation to discuss the issue in relation to African Americans and 'foreign' domestic labour.

Racisms of class

Hollands (1990) examines the types of racism adopted by class groups. He suggests a typology of different racisms across and **within** class, gender and age. He uses three class codes adopted by Phil Cohen in his work on antiracist youth work in schools (1986):

- **The aristocratic breeding code** – black and white are each bred into particular codes and differ physically, emotionally, intellectually.

- **The bourgeois/democratic scientific code** – supplementing the breeding code [above] with a biologically based justification centring on sexuality and the body.

- **The working class code** – emphasises the inheritance of labour power and skills and control over private and public territory (Hollands 1990; Mac an Ghaill 1999).

Research shows that working class white racism is not homogenous (Cohen 1997) and that it varies in strength according to place and time as well as in relation to gender and age. Cohen's research showed that there were differences in attitudes towards racism among the young men on the Youth Training Scheme. Those on schemes with better job prospects and with fewer young black trainees were more likely to have a *laissez faire* attitude to racism than other young men on the scheme because their relative privilege had been maintained. When these privileges were challenged there were cries that this was 'unfair' and a need to resort to 'appropriate' rules of behaviour. Where the prospects were less good for trainees, race was a highly charged issue and these white trainees resented being on schemes dominated by black young people. In their eyes, this confirmed that such schemes were rubbish. Such racisms may also be contradictory. The same people might support the racist immigration policies of the National Front, may also take an active part in concerts on rocking against racism and be involved in beating up black people.

Whilst working class racism has traditionally laid emphasis on territory and labour power as a means by which working class identity could be maintained, some commentators believe that middle class racism is more an exercise of choice (Wieivorka 1995: although this research focuses on France, the author maintains that his conclusions hold for Western Europe as a whole). This choice results in segregation from ethnic minority communities. Such racism has had been given virtually no attention when public policy is drawn up or training designed.

The middle classes are defined by participation in consumption, mobility and opportunities for going up in the world rather than dangers of going down. They have tried to mark themselves off not so much from poor manual workers as from the immigrant population, which they see as a threat to their ethnicity and religion. The middle classes have deserted certain areas and moved to homogenous suburbs. They have resorted to private education and taken their children out of schools with large minority populations. This creates ethnic segregation, which is itself imbued with racism. It has contributed indirectly to the rise of populism, which has found its chief expression in France in the Front National where racism is part of their platform. By operating on a logic based on segregation and keeping the racialised population at bay, the middle classes mark their distance from people who signify both social decline and a different racial identity. This builds the racialised group into a threat and a scapegoat.

Gendered racisms

Although there has been little focus on the gendered racisms of the white middle class, Mac an Ghaill's study researched the relationship of ethnic identity to whiteness among a group of English white middle class men. They defined themselves as the Real Englishmen and felt that the idea of a masculine English identity had declined or, rather, that there had been a demise of English culture:

> **Adam**: It's like we can't be English, English men, proud to be English. I argue about this with my dad all the time. He just dismisses it saying it's all constructed and we should all be internationalists.
>
> **MM**: Why is it important to you?
>
> **Adam**: Because it's unfair. All the Asian kids and the black kids, they can be Asian or black. They can be proud of their countries.
>
> **MM**: Do you think of yourselves as racist?
>
> **Adam**: No. No. That's what the teachers try and tell you, they try and force on you if you say anything; try to make you feel guilty like them. But we're not talking about colour. We're talking about culture.
>
> **Richard**: English culture. And if you talk about the English flag or whatever, anything to do with Englishness, they call you a little fascist. (Mac an Ghaill 1997 p.143-144).

Mac an Ghaill considers these views contradictory and ambivalent. The men's identities embraced new cultural forms of racism as well as contradictory forms of inherited imperial images. They did not want to address their own ethnic majority status but they did acknowledge the ethnicity of minorities. The research also demonstrated the reluctance of teachers to discuss Englishness. Mac an Ghaill suggests that the fragile construction of an Anglo ethnic identity becomes stabilised though educational and other institutions in our society to administrate and regulate the categories as somehow fixed. These young white men felt their experience in inner city schools was one of being bullied by both black and white working class students. They were disenchanted that school authorities did not view their experiences as racist.

Violent racism, nationalism and xenophobia are seen to be the prerogatives of young unemployed men whose 'natural aggressive' energies would once have been channelled into manual labour or legitimate warfare (Ware 1997). As a consequence, expressions of racism by white working class women have received minimal attention compared to those of their male counterparts. Yet Ware's study demonstrates the importance of addressing the femininised nature of racism. Femininity implies an instinctive loyalty to husbands and families through the implication of men's need to be collective. Focusing too closely on the masculinity associated with racism will mislead us in our understanding of how to counter it.

Ware (1997) explores the rise of the British National Party in 1993. After the general election of 1993, attacks against Bengalis rose. The perpetrators appeared to be white men in their 20s and 30s. However, Ware points out that white working class women, too, expressed their racism, referring to threats to the kinship amongst their families; to religious incompatibility; to Bangladeshis 'being unhygienic and bringing disease'. Bangladeshis in council houses were perceived to be jumping the housing queue because of their large families or by making themselves homeless. The white women appealed for families to be kept together, in one place. These views supposedly represent a 'feminine' point of view as they involve domestic space, smells, spitting, disease and all the things that are a threat to the home. Ware argues that women like these help present racism as a heartfelt appeal for justice, unlike the attitudes and actions of the 'macho racist thugs'. At the same time, the women's racism is contradictory. For example, the housing given to Bangladeshis was seen as undesirable by whites. The discourse among these women also evoked the 'old' racism of white supremacy, which is highly racialised and highly sexualised. For example, the women expressed fears about their safety and of being 'mugged by blacks'.

Kelly (1988) found that racist abuse and fights differed between boys and girls and also within each gender. She found that racial name-calling, teasing about dress and bullying took place between Asian and white girls and also between African Caribbean and Asian girls. The boys engaged in similar behaviour but were more likely to get involved in fights. There was also a much higher incidence of racial fights in all-boys' schools than in mixed schools.

Cohen's study demonstrates how white working class men use gendered and patriarchal characteristics to represent differing ethnic groups. They viewed young men of African Caribbean origin as 'macho', ' hard' or heavy' and Sikh Asians as 'wimps'.

In effect certain elements are selected from African Caribbean 'culture' and privileged because they are associated with the street code of manual working class masculinity; in contrast certain elements are selected from the Asian cultural heritage because they can be made to signify petty bourgeois and effeminate traits. (Cohen 1997 p.168).

Racisms across age and generation

Thus there are intra-class differences in relation to gender. But there are also intra-age and intra-ethnicity differences. For example, Mac an Ghaill's study of white working class young men showed how those who were upwardly mobile challenged the racism of their parents. They rejected their parents' views that, for example, black people were responsible for mass unemployment (Mac an Ghaill, 1999). Their racism took other forms.

Hewitt's study of young people in a predominantly white part of Greenwich explores the 'routes' of racism (1996). He shows that young men and women do not straightforwardly accept and take on the non-racist or racist language or views of their parents. For young men, in particular, their peer group is far more influential. It is through young male peer groups acting together that an individual may take the route from expressing racist abuse through engaging in vandalism and graffiti, and ultimately to attacking a young black man walking on his own through 'their' territory.

Tackling white racisms by intervention

According to recent research by Huddersfield University, very little antiracist educative youth work is carried out with potential perpetrators of racist crimes (*Connections* 1999). This research reveals that there is fear and ambivalence within youth work itself about working educatively with white youth. Working with racist youth is complicated by the fact that the route they take is not necessarily along a single path towards violence. Willems points out that young men differ and not all racist youths are violent. Different interventions are needed for different members of this group.

Where there has been antiracist work, it has largely focused on ethnic minorities. Working with white and black young people together is rare. The youth clubs that do have a policy on race are likely to ban racism. This silencing may be counterproductive to challenging racism. The Macdonald Inquiry showed how white students were simply expected to respect the cultures and beliefs of black peoples, however they felt about them. Without offering any mechanism for people to explore their own racist beliefs or feelings, such policies can lead to the entrenchment of racism and/or polarisation of white and black (Macdonald Inquiry 1989). The banning of racism can provide an entry route into the British National Party, as happened in South East London (Dadzie 1997; *Connections* 1999).

However, there are some isolated examples of innovative and effective interventions in tackling white racisms. These initiatives promoted educative work with young people primarily young men (e.g. Dadzie 1997: *Blood, Sweat and Tears*; Hewitt 1996; Institute of Education 1992). Recently, there have also been a number of anti-racist interventions within youth work itself (see National Youth Agency lists of antiracist projects July 1999). A conference, which was jointly funded by the CRE and the National Youth Agency called for more antiracist youth work (*Young People* Now, June 1999).

The Bede Anti Racist Youth Work Project intervened with the leaders and members of gangs of white working class men (Dadzie 1997), in response to a rising number of racist attacks in the local area of Bermondsey, and there were also interventions with young white women and young Somali men. In South East London racist attacks in the 1990s increased by 36% (*Connections* 1999). It was recognised that the intervention would need a long-term commitment, so resources were devoted and workers were recruited to the idea of challenging racism. This intervention would, it was agreed, take place in relation to the young people's lived and everyday experience. Team meetings of youth workers developed strategies for racist feelings to be openly discussed. They discussed, for example, how to ensure that young people viewed the black youth worker as a positive role model. She was placed in a decision-making role in many discussions with the young people, and other workers deferred to her, openly admiring her style. The young people also analysed and discussed how racism is embedded and how it produces and reproduces itself. Racism was explicitly discussed, but not *artificially* placed on the agenda. On many occasions it was not discussed at all; it was raised only at strategic moments. The evaluation of the project showed interesting results. Young white people who had been aggressively racist in their views and behaviour started to opt out when their friends made racist comments. One year later, many of the 200 young people said the project had changed their lives. Racist incidents on the estate where the project operated reduced by 46% over three years, whereas they increased as a whole in Bermondsey.

The Bede project also found that some girls were more self aware and less aggressive than the boys. They were less influenced by peer group pressure and more receptive to antiracist ideas. The girls could be useful in challenging the racism of the boys, but only when they felt secure and confident in their ability to make decisions in their lives that related to their position as *girls*.

Professional power and racism

A myth has developed that those who occupy the professions do not serve their own interests, adhering to codes of ethics, neutrality, and altruism for their clients (Esland 1980). However, it can be argued that professionals perform a gatekeeper role in the distribution of society's material and social resources. They use the idea of 'autonomy' to conceal decisions made behind closed doors. Their clients have little access to information as to how decisions are made. The professional societies are supposedly neutral and independent, but are usually run by the professionals themselves. They thus control access to the profession and plan their own training.

This autonomy of the professions has yet to be directly challenged, although it has been placed under scrutiny by the development of a managerial agenda, which emphasises the importance of accountability and efficiency (Davies, 2000). The professional cloak of secrecy legitimates the racialised and gendered power structures of exclusion in wider society. Occupational culture can refer to the values, norms and patterns of action, which characterize social relationships within a particular occupation. There is little research on professional occupational cultures and professional power and racism. Research on psychiatrists, teachers and the police helps us to see the kind of racism that may be exercised by those in positions of professional power.

Psychiatrists

There is evidence that psychiatrists practice their racism within their professional realm. Certain groups are associated with certain disorders e.g. disproportionately high numbers of Caribbean origin males are diagnosed as schizophrenic. Different groups are differentially stereotyped, and this is followed by applying different methods of control. For example, Caribbean origin male patients are more likely to be locked in wards, diagnosed as violent and put in secure units. They are three times more likely to be admitted and detained under the 1983 Mental Health Act. South Asian origin women are disproportionately more likely to be diagnosed as hysterical (Smaje 1995). These decisions, made by psychiatrists, are then ascribed to cultural differences in behaviour. Greater transparency in the interactions between patients and psychiatrists may provide clues to how to intervene in training programmes to challenge racism. Autonomously made, scientifically based judgements must themselves be interrogated in order for such racist processes to be effectively challenged.

Teachers

Teachers often adopt a colour-blind neutral rhetoric, but frequently behave in ways that disadvantage black or other minority students (Gillborn 1997). Teachers have long been seen as dedicated members of a profession that encourages all children to reach their potential. Teachers can stereotype different groups in differing ways. Students of South Asian origin are affected by teachers misreading their bilingual skills. Teachers have scant regard for a child's fluency in their community language or languages, and view their possible lesser proficiency in English as a learning difficulty. Teachers view African Caribbean students as likely to be disruptive or to present other disciplinary problems (Gillborn, 1997 p.6) and make assumptions about their criminality, lack of motivation and low ability (Gillborn Youdell and Kirton 1997; Sewell 1997). The occupational culture of teachers is '*implicit in staffroom cultures towards black boys and towards non-Western traditions and heritages, particularly Islam*' (Richardson 1999 p. 9). Richardson points out that the Ofsted Report on *Raising the attainment of ethnic minority pupils* (10

March 1999) makes no reference to teachers' occupational culture and manages to discuss at length the underachievement of black boys without once mentioning the fearful attitudes and low expectations of them held by many teachers. Similarly, it points to the underachievement of Pakistani and Bangladeshi pupils without once referring to the Islamophobia which exists in the teaching profession, as it does in wider society (Richardson 1999 p. 9).

The Police

The history of policing with regard to black people has been well documented over the last thirty years. Gilroy has argued that this history is intimately connected with the changing forms, methods and aims of policing under crisis conditions and thus to their changed occupational culture (1983).

In the mid-1960s, breakdowns in relations between black people and the police were put down to mutual misunderstandings in official discourse. But in the 1970s things began to change. On the one hand, authors such as Gus John began to document police racist practices and behaviour (Gilroy 1982). On the other, there was a greater construction of crime in relation to specific groups; new crimes in the 1970s, such as 'mugging', were associated with black people. Media commentary in relation to race was dominated by the continuing construction of black young people as lawless and this was conflated with the threat of 'illegal' immigrants, fuelled by repressive immigration and nationality laws (Hall *et al* 1978; Gilroy 1982; Bunyan 1981). Social instability in inner cities increasingly became identified with the growing confrontations between the police and working class organisations, combined with better organisation by groups of black young people – both African Caribbean and later Asian – protesting at their treatment by the police (Gilroy 1982).

From the 1960s on, the police force itself was subject to much change through increasing professionalisation and specialisation. This impacted on relationships between the police and black people. Law and order campaigns launched by the Police Federation made the connection between geographical areas, class and black people. The Special Patrol Group – the 'force within a force' – adopted a military style and philosophy and was often armed. Great emphasis was placed on being prepared, acting swiftly and with great mobility. SPG units were often used in 'swamping operations' in Brixton, Handsworth and elsewhere, amplifying the relationship between black young people and lawlessness (Hall et al 1978).

These changes in the police role and the subsequent racialisation of actions by the force reinforced the particular nature of police organisational cultures – command and control, entrenched racism, militarism (Gilroy 1983:143 and 145). The introduction of various equal opportunity measures, such as training after the 1981 disturbances and the subsequent Scarman Report, failed to impact on this deep-seated culture. The dominant discourse of the media and government in response to the disturbances was to further criminalize black young people and to suggest their behaviour was culturally alien (Gilroy 1987; Sivanandan 1986; West Midlands County Council 1986).

Gilroy exposes a vast catalogue of police malpractice in their dealings with black people starting from a report in 1965, presented to the West Indian Standing Conference and entitled 'Nigger Hunting in England', right up to the 1980s (Gilroy 1982). Below is one example:

> Superintendent Dick Holland of the West Yorkshire CID, for example, having cited young West Indian 'muggers' as his illustration, ...said: 'Police must be prejudiced if they are to do their job properly'. An unnamed inspector stationed at Brixton explained to the *Daily Mail* that the operational vocabulary of his men had been extended during the riots from the words 'Coon, Sooty, Spade, which like other four letter words in industrial language [sic] are something blokes working together will say without meaning a thing' to include habitual use of words like 'nigger'.' (Gilroy 1983 p.144-5)

More recently, the recruitment and retention of black police officers has received a great deal of attention. From black officers who leave the force and take their case to an industrial tribunal we hear about everyday racist language and abuse in the police force. They report being called 'sambo', 'jungle bunny', 'coon' 'nigger'; being refused promotion because of skin colour, and they make general allegations of racial discrimination (Murji and Cutler 1990).

Holdaway (2000) argues there is a huge gap between policy intentions in the police force and the ways these are negated, changed or ignored as we go down the chain of command. The occupational culture which legitimates a discretionary freedom in everyday police work is allowed to be interpreted as 'police common sense'. This then becomes the norm. The police occupational culture is strongly related to ideas about race. Many officers use negative derogatory language when talking about black people as a matter of course – it has been identified as part of their 'canteen culture'. This is not restricted to relationships with black colleagues.

> By policing normally, in what officers regard as 'common sense' ways, and failing to reflect on the implications of their ideas and actions, negative relationships between the police and ethnic minorities are created and sustained. (Holdaway 2000)

A Nottinghamshire Audit found that sergeants and constables overall were openly hostile to admitting to racism, and believed that positive discrimination was commonplace. They remembered the days when banter could flow freely. They argued that the Anglo-Saxon male was under threat and that ethnic minorities had too much power (Nottinghamshire Police 2000). Civilian staff in Nottinghamshire Police allege sexist and racist language is used in their canteens (Nottinghamshire Police Audit 1999). The Gifford Report (1989) concluded that wholly unacceptable racist language and behaviour was common among officers of rank in the Merseyside Police. Holdaway (2000) reveals that many officers used derogatory language when talking about black people, and that this was not restricted to relationships with black colleagues. A conference in Swindon in 1998 on Visible Women, heard from a member of the black police officers association that name-calling, harassment and offensive behaviour were prevalent in the police force. Black police officers felt isolated, excluded and marginalised (Swindon REC 1998).

Holdaway (2000) found that those at the highest levels in the police force failed to understand the notion of positive action and the relevance of race to policing. Two aspects sustain this culture: the lack of political will to counter racism at the highest levels and an overwhelmingly white masculinised culture, which is reinforced in large peer groups and goes unchallenged.

Such studies show that there are embedded occupational cultures of deep-seated racism, expressed within a variety of organisational cultures of institutions. Racism is about relationships between groups, based on power. Accordingly, all groups have to be involved in addressing challenging it.

Conclusion

Racisms of class, gender, age, occupation, ethnicity, and specificity of stereotyping of different ethnic groups suggests that an entirely new approach to training is required. The specificity of the racism and its local reproduction, together with dominant discourse, must be examined in their micro and macro contexts. Once viewed in this way, it becomes clear that racism cannot be challenged in a generalised fashion. Off-the-shelf, add-on training looks increasingly irrelevant.

In order to intervene in racism effectively, there has to be a longer-term analysis of how racism is embedded in specific contexts and cultures and how it is expressed. This is crucial to designing training or educational interventions. Off-the-shelf training courses on cultural differences or a racism awareness day are likely to have little or no effect in challenging racism.

This ineffectiveness will be further demonstrated in the the next chapter's analysis of the transcripts of the Stephen Lawrence Inquiry. By examining discourse, or the police 'talk' about racism, we may be in a better position to appreciate the difficulties of designing just one training programme to combat racism. As the examination reveals, the police occupational culture has specific and widely used strategies for denying racism. When someone denies racism, they argue rationally, for example, that racism does not exist in the police force, yet internally or unconsciously, they realise that it does. Furthermore, whilst denying racism, the police reveal themselves to hold misconceptions about race. These misconceptions are embedded in police occupational culture and in other institutions and professions. It is these misconceptions and the denial of racism which must be tackled.

4

Discourse Theory and Police Evidence from the Stephen Lawrence Inquiry

Introduction

In the 1960s and 1970s many committed activists focused on the *structures* which perpetuate racism. In the late 1980s and 1990s, a wealth of writing in academia on cultural forms and processes has influenced theoretical work on the changing conceptions of racism. It was argued that material structures and processes were not the only ways in which racism was reproduced and there was a consequent 'turn to culture' and a new interest in cultural production and the politics of identity (Solomos and Back 1996). Studies on racialised discourses in the media or popular culture examined the changing images of representation in the popular media, film and historical literature. Study of the creation and reproduction of racialised images and representation in cultural forms, notably language, has led to a growing interest in examining language as a site for the reproduction of inequality.

Attention to the processes of racism has gone side by side with attention to the language of racism – its expression and reproduction through discourse. Analysis of the language of racism has, however, *not* been carried out in relation to racist practice, since scholars and researchers see themselves as liberal and tolerant. They criticise the discourse analysis approach as being too exaggerated, ridiculous and 'political' (van Dijk 1999). This is particularly interesting when the history of racism is riddled with scholars and scientists who have been allowed to write, debate and sell their work legitimating black inferiority as if it were an objective topic.

However, by understanding the conditions and consequences of such talk and texts we may be able to locate and analyse them in social interactions. Racist discourses need to be rigorously contextualised and situated in specific political, cultural, social and economic moments. Different racisms may be expressed through a classed, gendered, nationalist position. These racisms are then reproduced through everyday talk about race and racism.

Several European studies have been made of multiculturalism and racist immigration discourse (Wimmer 1997), which argue that holders of semi-official or official power use the discourse of difference and culture to exclude the 'other'. They then institutionalise this exclusion in their social policy. In this way, their own politics are not subject to scrutiny, since the blame for impoverishment and exclusion has been made to lie in cultural distinctiveness. Van Dijk (1993) maintains that racist discourse is reproduced by multiple acts of exclusion and marginalisation. Ideology and a set of attitudes that legitimate difference and dominance sustain these acts. In some countries, such as the Netherlands, the term racism is only applied to the expressions of right-wing extremists. As long as the other manifestations of racism are denied, there is no need for official measures to combat them. There is no need to review regulations and processes and no need for moral campaigns to change the biased attitudes of whites. Overt expressions of racism are inconsistent with norms of equality and the democratic humanitarianism of present-day society:

> To manage such contradictions, white speakers engage in strategies of positive self-presentation in order to be able credibly to present the 'others' in a negative light. (van Dijk 1993 p.193)

Paying attention to the language of racism helps to reveal other kinds of racisms. How white people, particularly, talk about racism may be useful in designing effective educational interventions. Their discourse may expose the racisms of power and powerlessness and the importance of strategic change in tackling educational training interventions to combat racism.

One way to map micro racisms through discourse is to examine the discourse of those who are not normally under scrutiny in relation to racism – in this case, white police officers. Analysis of the transcripts of the Stephen Lawrence Inquiry provides a case study of discourse on racism as expressed by police officers at different levels of the police hierarchy. The following analysis examines some of the opening speeches of the lawyers acting for the various parties but it focuses most closely on the words of the police officers. The analysis is drawn mainly from Part I of the Inquiry and Sir Paul Condon's evidence in Part II.

Methodology

Twenty-one transcripts of evidence are analysed according to how witnesses speak about race and racism. Officers in the following hierarchical levels of the police gave evidence:

> Police Constables (23)
> Police Sergeants (11)
> Police Inspectors (10)
> Police Superintendents (10)
> Assistant Commissioners and the Commissioner (6)

A random sample of six was selected from the first category and four each from the following three categories. In addition the evidence from Assistant Commissioner Johnston, Acting Commissioner Nove and the Commissioner, Paul Condon is examined. Below is a list of the witnesses – the cast of characters named in the analysis.

Cast of Characters

Inquiry Team
Sir William Macpherson of Cluny, Chairman to the Inquiry
Dr Richard Stone
Mr Tom Cook
The Right Reverend Dr John Sentamu, Bishop of Stepney

The Lawyers

Edmund Lawson QC, counsel to the Inquiry
Michael Mansfield QC, counsel to the Lawrence family
Stephen Kamlish, led by Mr Mansfield
Jeremy Gompertz QC, counsel for the Commissioner of the Metropolitan Police
Mr Imran Khan, solicitor for the Lawrence family

The Witnesses
Police Constable Joanne Smith
Police Constable Anthony Gleason
Police Constable Nigel Clements
Detective Constable Steven Pye
Detective Constable Michael Tomlin
Detective Constable Christopher Budgen
Detective Constable Linda Holden
Detective Sergeant Christopher Crowley
Detective Sergeant David Cooper
Detective Inspector Benjamin Bullock
Detective Inspector Steven Groves
Detective Inspector John Bevan
Detective Inspector Philip Jeynes
Inspector Ian Little
Detective Superintendent William Mellish
Detective Superintendent Jonathan McIvor
Detective Superintendent Ian Crampton
Detective Chief Superintendent John Barker
Assistant Commissioner Ian Johnston
Acting Commissioner Perry Nove
Commissioner Sir Paul Condon
Duwayne Brooks, friend of Stephen Lawrence

Comments on the analysis

The Stephen Lawrence Inquiry was held in public. White police officers across differing ranks appeared before a number of lawyers representing the Lawrences, the Metropolitan Police, Duwayne Brooks and the Inquiry Panel itself. All the witnesses were under intense public scrutiny. They had not only to account for their actions and management of the investigations into the murder but had also to speak out in public about race and racism in a way they would almost certainly not have done before.

Thus it is difficult to read from their remarks what an unguarded rambling of thoughts and feelings by white Police officers on race and racism might have sounded like. The discussions were taking place in an atmosphere where overt racism was not acceptable or legitimate, particularly in the public eye. In an atmosphere of this kind, words are subject to intense censure. In addition, it is certain that witnesses will plan with colleagues in advance what they are going to say. Patterns in the talk may well have been planned beforehand. The kind of questions asked would need to catch witnesses off guard, so that concealed thoughts and feelings could be revealed. Not all the lawyers achieved such revelations. Nevertheless, it is possible to identify nuances, silences, and coded racisms in the evidence that tell us a good deal about the discourse and nature of racism.

Opening remarks of the inquiry

Mr. Lawson, Counsel to the Inquiry, opens his remarks by stating clearly that the murder was racist (Day 2 p.47). This is affirmed by other members of the Inquiry: Tom Cook speaks of the 'racist' murder of Stephen Lawrence (p.26) so do Richard Stone (p.29) and Bishop Sentamu (the attack was '*demonstrably racist*') (Day 2 p.35).

The opening remarks by the lawyers and panel members set the tone for the talk about the murder – that it was indeed racist. As the lawyers continue, two key issues in racism talk are revealed.

Firstly, the lawyers vary in their understanding of racism. Although Edmund Lawson says the murder was '*plainly racist*' (Day 2 p.100), he links this with individual motive: '*it is repellent that anybody who commits a murder should get away with it and anyone who does so and murders for racist motives and should escape is doubly repellent*' (Day 2 p.100). In other words, he is connecting individual intentional (presumably conscious) racism with Stephen's murder. This may indeed be true but the use of one word to describe both the intention and structures/ideology is confusing. A distinction should be made between racism and racialism. The Macdonald Inquiry ten years earlier provided clear definitions that clarify that distinction:

> A murder may be properly described as racialist if it is done for a racialist motive, out of racial prejudice, for example if the victim was black.

> A murder may be racist if the culture and context in which the killing takes place mirrors the relative positions in society of black and white people or reflects the racist hierarchy in which we live and perceive ourselves. (Macdonald Inquiry 1989 p. 44)

The distinction between conscious intentional racist motives and the culture, structures and hierarchies of racism needs to be made clear. Conflating racism with racialism makes it impossible for individuals to deny racialism while accepting racism. It seems clear, however, that the murder of Stephen Lawrence was both racist and racialist.

Secondly, the Counsel to the Inquiry uses the word 'race' in a way that separates the issue from the context of society. He says the Inquiry will consider whether issues of race affected any or all of the issues to be considered (Day 2 p.102). He fails to understand that race as a social construction is *part* of British society. As earlier chapters in this study have demonstrated, race does not just concern black people. The historical and political relationship between different racialised groups produces the structures under which we all live. To ask whether race is an issue is to elicit the inevitable answer, yes. It is more important to consider how racism itself is manifest in the case under scrutiny.

Also significant is the use of Mr. Lawson's use of the word '*racial*', in relation to the Unit at Plumstead Station called the *Racial* Incidents Unit (Day 2 p.103), where the term *racial* rather than *racist* attacks is customarily used. But Mr. Lawson appears to use the words *race, racial* and *racist* interchangeably here. He uses *race* primarily to identify blackness and whiteness and racial for a relationship *between* black and white, but neither embraces the relationship of power to the operation of racism. In common usage *race* and *racial* are based on phenotypical features, primarily skin colour, and are often not seen as related to the social construction of racism as power. This concealed power relationship is then reflected in the structures and processes of society. It may be worth emphasising that racism existed before the construction of notions of race or racial.

Mr Mansfield, QC, Counsel for the Lawrence family, introduces the word *unconscious* into the investigation: '*racism, both conscious and unconscious, permeated the investigation*' (Day 2 p.118) and says that the killing of Stephen was '*racist*'. He suggests that racism is not singular in focus when he describes racists as interested in directing their venom only at the black or Jewish population, while he highlights how the expressions of everyday racialist remarks are based on dominant discourse. He recalls the remark of the woman who told Doreen Lawrence that her son would not have been killed if: '*he had not been there*' and links this remark to the speeches of politicians who express the same sentiment in the context of immigration and the presence of black people in Britain (Day 2 p.120). He displays some understanding of racism and its usage, since he links everyday expressions of racism with dominant or government discourse. Such a link legitimates the acceptability of racism in everyday language. At the same time, he often uses terms such as the '*forces of racism*' as if racism were beyond human agency.

Mr Gompertz, the lawyer for the Metropolitan Police, believes that race and racism are something 'out there' (Day 2 p.147). He associates racism with '*wickedness*' (p.147) and asks how we can remove this '*blight*' (a disease?). Racism is defined as an 'evil', a disease to be eradicated, rather than as something embedded in the very nature of modern British society and the way it has been formed.

Mr Gompertz denies police racism but admits that the police committed errors: '*... it is quite possible to be highly motivated and to try hard, but to get things wrong. That is human nature. It is also quite possible to get things wrong, perhaps even very wrong, without being racist and without being in any way influenced by conscious or subconscious feelings of antipathy towards certain individuals or groups*' (Day 2 p.149-150). According to Mr Gompertz, the police cannot be racist because they are not evil or wicked or even 'callous' (p.150). This conception of racism allows him to deny its existence and attribute its operation to human errors. Sir Paul Condon echoes this conception when he talks about racism as a 'peril' or 'evil' (Part II p. 302). This strategy of positive self-presentation and denial by the elite not only saves face but also helps avoid negative public impressions in an atmosphere where overt racism is condemned (Van Djik 1993).

Mr Gompertz suggests that the errors made by the police were 'human nature':

> The police officers involved in this case are all different personalities. They have different backgrounds and live in different circumstances.

They have children of their own; some hold deeply religious and personal beliefs. In short, they are individuals capable of feeling grief and being upset like anybody else. They are not robots. They have been angered and upset that Stephen's killers have not been brought to justice. They are also deeply concerned that they have been portrayed as callous racists. Those allegations have affected not only the officers but also their families who have been upset by this unfair labelling of their loved ones (Day 2 p.150).

Van Dijk suggests that the expression of such 'in-group allegiance' and white solidarity defends 'us' against 'them': *'They mark social boundaries and reaffirm social and ethnic identities and self attribute moral superiority to their own group'* (van Dijk 1993 p. 181).

The denial of racism

The denial of racism permeates the transcripts of evidence given by the police. There is a clearly discernible pattern of disclaimers of racism and a huge unwillingness to discuss it explicitly. The key ways in which this denial is manifest are through silence about the subject; a sudden loss of memory; and an unwillingness to acknowledge that racism exists. Although some of this silence is due to the public nature of the Inquiry and the resulting scrutiny of the Metropolitan Police, there is a sense in which the definition of racism by the Metropolitan Police lawyer Mr Gompertz as explicit, overt and evil, conditions the police responses. Some questions in the Inquiry tended to be asked rationally and directly, e.g. *did you stereotype Duwayne Brooks?* and these led to immediate denial. Such denial is evident also in answers to other questions in which police officers are asked if they acted in a racist manner.

The meaning of racism is changed and redefined for 'common sense' use by the police officers. Almost all the police officers have no idea what racism means, nor do they try to interpret its meaning. They may refer to racism as something to do with inner cities and black people; as being about *individual* unchanging attitudes that originate in white people and are expressed towards black people; as being about understanding cultures. Their misconceptions about racism allow them to deny its existence. All the transcripts examined contain denials of racism but these denials take different forms.

Senior officers use denial in a slightly different way to the junior officers. There follows what can be described as a typology of denial.

1. Denial as personal racism

All the ten police constables and sergeants whose evidence I examined dismissed racism as being despicable. They felt it was insulting to be asked whether they should be labelled as racist. Police Constable Joanne Smith's response is typical, when she says she finds it 'insulting' to be called racist. This response is undoubtedly conditioned by the fact that she perceives the police officers as being bracketed with the suspects in the use of the terminology 'racist'. Junior officers such as constables and sergeants use a variety of strategies to deny their personal racism. Some resort to the same ploy as the lawyer for the Metropolitan Police and assert their positive self-presentation and moral superiority:

> We have black people in our church that we mix with and they are brothers, if you like, of mine, and it is not something that ... I just totally refute that. I mean it is just crazy (Police Constable Geddis p. 380 Day 3).

Assistant Commissioner Johnston is asked about his understanding of the facts that suggest the investigation of the murder was racist. He treats this as an allegation that individual officers were discriminating intentionally:

> Q. If you are, what therefore gives you the impression that it might not be a possibility that racism is playing a part? If you have taken seriously their reasons, have you advanced other contrary reasons — because I am not hearing that? All I am hearing is moving on in the future.
>
> A. Right, right. I think we are into perceptions that we have to address in handling racial crimes and in handling our interface with the community. I think what I am saying is that the intentions of those officers was not racist, that they were doing what they thought was right; although I think that Mr Kamlish has been trying to lay out why inadequacies in training, inadequacies in support could have underpinned that. I don't think that they were looking — I really don't think they were looking at Stephen and saying: "We are not going to help him, because he is a black child'. I really don't think that, sir. I have

worked in the Metropolitan Police for a long while, and I know this doesn't go down well with the gallery, but I do not believe it, sir. (p.8723)

Thus a denial of overt intentional racism (racialism) is offered in response to the question about whether racism has played a part. Assistant Commissioner Johnson argues that police officers were not intentionally and consciously racist, as there is no explicit evidence that they are. He shows no awareness about covert, unconscious racism nor the slightest understanding of the cultural context of racism.

2. Denials and counter attacks

Once a more positive image of the police force is constructed, as in Mr Gompertz's opening remarks and those by the officer above, senior officers can subtly deny their own responsibility for racism. This was the line taken by the Commissioner, Sir Paul Condon, when he elaborated on the denial of 'institutional racism'. He suggested that labelling the police as racist would, in effect, deny how well intentioned and sincere most police officers are:

I have serious reservations for the future of these important issues if the expression "institutional racism" is used in a particular way. I am not in denial. I am not seeking weasel words. I have been the first to be critical of police officers and the police service to say things which are unpopular. I am not denying the challenge or the need for reform, but if you label, if this Inquiry labels my service as "institutionally racist" (pause), then the average police officer, the average member of the public will assume the normal meaning of those words. They will assume a finding of conscious detriment of ethnic minority Londoners. They will assume the majority of good men and women who come into policing to serve their fellow men go home to their families; go to their churches; go to their voluntary groups; go about their daily lives with racism in their minds and in their endeavour. I actually think that use of those two words in a way that would take on a new meaning to most people in society would actually undermine many of the endeavours to identify and respond to the issues of racism which challenge all institutions and particularly the police because of their privileged and powerful position. (Part 2 p.290)

Later he reiterates the fact that police officers are: *'well meaning, intelligent people'* (p.308) and any collective idea of institutional racism would be difficult to 'acknowledge'.

As well as this positive self-presentation, racism is denied by placing the problem of racism on black people themselves or on the general public – or anyone but the police. Take this extract from Assistant Commissioner Johnston's evidence:

Q. Thank you. I would like to go back to the way in which he was treated as a victim. You have told this Inquiry about the high standards you expect your officers to treat victims, and you have accepted that Mr Brooks was not treated that way. He feels that he was not treated that way because he was a young black man. Now, it is right, is it not, Mr Johnston, that his perception of how he was treated is consistent or follows a pattern with a lot of young black men who fall into the hands of the Metropolitan Police? They feel that the police treat them not as victims, but as suspects. That is right, is it not?

A. I accept the general point that a number of young black men have negative perceptions of the police service. Of course I accept that point.

Q. And they are, on the whole, right, are they not? Just as Mr Brooks was not treated as a victim, there are many such young black men who are not treated as victims, when they are in fact victims?

A. I am not going to sit here and say that we do not, from time to time, treat black people badly; nor, from time to time, do we treat white people badly. I do accept that there is enormous importance in treating black people properly and fairly and generously. It is difficult for me to go from that position to agreeing about specific numbers of black people. I don't draw back from the claim that there is a significant problem of confidence in the police service amongst black young men.

Q. Did you say 'confidence'?

A. Yes. It is a challenge for us to overcome. (p.8759-8760)

Here the Assistant Commissioner neatly turns the way in which young black men are treated and stereotyped by the police into a construction which places the onus on them to regain confidence in the police. He implies that these young men are mistaken because from time to time, both black people and white are treated badly by the police.

The questioner continues to pursue the treatment of black young men by the Police:

Q. I want to turn from young black men's perceptions of the police to your analysis of how the police treat young black victims of crime. Do you accept that there is a pattern of the police not treating young black victims of crime as victims of crime; do you accept that?

A. It is very difficult for me to say. Again, I am not trying to draw back from the suggestion. I mean, of course there are documented cases where we have let people down; and I am not in any sense being dismissive in saying I regret that and that is wrong. But to go from there to statements of generalities about truth, I think I can't make that leap. I can accept, and accept that the challenges for us to overcome, that there are negative perceptions of the way that black people are treated by the police service. There are stereotypes of police officers. There are stereotypes of most people, some of which carry some truth, some of which do not. It is the challenge for the police service, and not for others, to overcome these issues, I accept. But I think there are real lessons around Mr Brooks. I don't think we recognise in the full sense that we would today – and therein lines the value of these types of events – about the need for treating him with more sensitivity. I don't then say that takes us into treating him in an overtly racist way. I think the debate is around, and we have had the debate already, around the more subtle forms of racism.

Q. So, you accept that he was treated in a covertly racist way, do you?

A. No, I don't accept that. I accept that there is a legitimate interpretation of that which the panel will obviously consider, and rightly consider and properly consider. (p.8760-8761)

When pushed, Commissioner Johnson moves away from placing the responsibility on to young black men. Implicit within his denial is the notion that the situation is not amenable to facts and evidence. It is a case of needing to change perceptions. Racism is neatly made to look like a case of individual differences, where everyone is guilty of stereotyping one another. The specific issue of the way young African Caribbean origin men are treated as lawless criminals is subtly dismissed.

Another mechanism is to counterattack by implying that whites are treated unfairly too. Junior officers in particular use this method. There is an assumption that treating a murder as a 'racist' murder implies favouritism to black people. So, as Inspector Little says:

> A murder is a murder is a murder. All of them are equally terrible. I don't think one should be given a higher category than another. Everyone should be treated the same. If everyone is equal they should be treated as such. (p. 1979)

This idea of reverse discrimination, i.e. favouring blacks against whites, is implicit in his argument. It forms part of the reason for the Inspector's denial. He argues that the interpretation of the murder as racist was not his but other people's. Resistance to 'special treatment' and 'reverse discrimination' are common tactics used in dialogue by people who have no understanding about the histories of racism or how it is maintained and reproduced through relationships of power and subordination.

3. Conscious denial in the face of overwhelming evidence of racism

The Inquiry highlighted the stereotyping of Duwayne Brooks as a 'troublemaker' with stereotyped characteristics associated with African Caribbean origin men. Detective Inspector Jeynes took over as senior officer for the investigation until Detective Superintendent Crampton came in as the first Senior Investigating Officer. The following forms part of Detective Inspector Jeynes' evidence.

> **Q** 'During my dealings with Duwayne Brooks', you are supposed to either cross out, notice or did not notice, 'that he displayed normal or abnormal, out of the ordinary behaviour.' According to you, during the time that you saw him at the police station, you noticed that he displayed abnormal or out of the ordinary behaviour. Do you remember this?
>
> **A**. I don't remember this at all, sir, no.
>
> Q. If you look at it further down. It says, I think that word is, 'surly and non-co-operative'. Do you remember this?
>
> **A**. No, sir.

Q. You see the date, 16th May 1994. Is that an accurate description of your recollection of Duwayne Brooks's behaviour at the police station?

A. I remember thinking he was angry, which is understandable.

Q. Yes?

A. Whether somebody had put — I mean, I really, honestly, I don't remember this at all. I just can't recall it.

Q That's the description that you give; is that right?

A. Yes, sir.

Q. A young man is somewhat disorderly, somewhat aggressive. That's what you seem to be describing here, is it not?

A. What I am saying is that he was getting up and walking out and was agitated and was angry, that is what I am describing.

Q. Causing a lot of problems and aggravation?

A. Yes, it was problems and aggravation for the DC who was trying to take the statement from the principal witness.

Q. We move on now from surly and non-co-operative to agitated, angry, causing problems and aggravation? Let us see what DC Cooper had to say about this matter. PCA 30, 138. Mr Jeynes, this is the statement of DC Cooper dated 3rd June of last year. This is what DC Cooper has to say about it: P-2279: "I would say that Duwayne was remarkably together considering what had happened. He was quite perceptive as to what was about to happen with regards to me taking a statement. I would say that he was an intelligent youth." That is how DC Cooper, the interviewing officer, describes Duwayne Brooks. No mention of angry or agitated or causing problems, awkward, causing aggravation, nothing of the kind. Do you see that?' (p.2274)

When reminded of the fact that he had written certain negative comments about Duwayne Brooks, despite the assessment of two other officers who found him intelligent and his behaviour normal, Inspector Jeynes cannot be budged from his view:

Q. Do you think that perhaps you were racially stereotyping Duwayne Brooks?

A. No, not at all.

Despite any rational attempt to persuade otherwise, stereotyping can always be denied, since it is subtle, unconscious and difficult to establish tangibly in a one-off encounter. If stereotyping is going to be tackled in training or education it has to be done in a subliminal way or across differing ethnic groups, including white. Rational attempts to persuade people they are mistaken are of negligible value, as the above interaction shows.

The premise that one can 'show the truth through evidence' is not always possible to accomplish when dealing with a culture which legitimises racism as a norm. This is illustrated by a statement made by Assistant Commissioner Johnston when asked about his view of Sir Paul Condon's statements about young black people being 'muggers':

> **Q**. The Commissioner's statement, made there on the 8th July 1995 says: 'It is a fact that many of the perpetrators of muggings are very young, black people who have been excluded from school and/or are unemployed.'
>
> **A**. Yes.
>
> **Q**. That was the statement that caused all the trouble. Then it was discovered that, subsequently, and reported in the *Sunday Times* on 9th July 1995, that the survey to which he referred which led to him to make those remarks only looked at black areas of inner cities where there was high black population of the inner cities, which means the statistics were effectively, certainly misleading Sir Paul, but misleading overall?
>
> **A**. No, that's not correct, sir. They looked at data across the whole of the Metropolitan Police.
>
> **Q**. The fact is the figures have been discredited since he made the statement, have they not?
>
> **A**. I don't think so.
>
> **Q**. It is not true, is it, that the perpetrators, the rate of perpetration of muggings in London, or indeed anywhere else, is highly — a high amount of them are young black people? It is not right to say that, is it?

A. I don't accept that. I would want to enter into a detailed explanation of this issue, sir, but I don't know how you want to me deal with it.

Q. We can't go into it now?

A. I don't accept it, but I'm not trying to be dismissive in not accepting it. (p.8706-8707)

Two lines later the transcripts reveal:

Mr Kamlish: I am not going to go on, but you have accepted the damage this statement did to race relations?

A. No, I am not accepting that. I am accepting that the media coverage of it damaged race relations.

Assistant Commissioner Johnston constantly denies any suggestion of racism or damage to race relations, but never once confronts the evidence which is staring him in the face.

4. Denial of the racist nature of the murder because of ideas of what is 'normal'

The obvious racist aspects of the murder were not explored by any police officers investigating on the evening of the murder or even weeks later. How should this capacity to ignore overt racism be explained? It may be that the culture accepts as the norm the representation of black people as criminalized; as inferior; as being subject to racial abuse. This may explain the fact that the police, and their refusal to take seriously the implications of racist crime, ignored the comment: 'what what nigger'. Although acknowledgement of the racist murder slowly makes its way up the hierarchy (two superintendents acknowledge racism in the murder, as does the Commissioner), Inspector Jeynes is one of a long line of police officers at middle and junior level (all Detective Constables, Inspectors, and Sergeants) who deny the racist aspects of the murder.

Questioner: did you consider at the time that this was a racially motivated, I will be precise, at the time you say are you the Senior Investigating Officer having arrived there at 12.15 up to 1.45, did you consider during that time that it was a racially motivated crime?

A. Not immediately sir, no.

Q. Just remember what you said already today. Did you consider at any time during that period that there was at possibility that this was a racially motivated crime?

A. There was a lot of possibilities.

Q. Sorry, just answer the questions?

A. No. I didn't.

Q. You did not?

A. No, not right away.

Q. Please do not get aggressive. Mr Jeynes, the question I asked is between 12.15 and 1.45. Did you consider during that time that it was a racially motivated crime?

A. I did not right away Sir. (p.2177-2178)

Inspector Jeynes doesn't know how to explain his lack of awareness. When the attitudes to which he subscribes are part of everyday culture, the norm, it is difficult to see them as out of the ordinary or 'abnormal'.

Inspector Little behaves according to the same pattern. He did not discuss the possibility of a racist attack with the Lawrences because he did not consider it relevant (p.1939). This strategy of denial is a variant: refusing to see something as 'different' from the norm, because to him, *it is the norm*. This attitude is confirmed by a night nurse in her comments upon the relaxed approach the police adopt to racist attacks. She worked in the hospital where Stephen was taken:

Q. A reason for your being called, Miss Lavin, is because of an observation you made on the second page of your statement, which is on the screen. The sentence beginning about five or six lines down: 'I think it true to say that victims of racially motivated attacks did present to our accident and emergency department on a regular basis. It is also true to say that on occasion I felt a general sense of unease about the police approach to such attacks in that the police tended to assume that such attacks were drugs related and, therefore, of less importance than other assaults'?

A. Yes, that is correct (Lavin Day 7 p. 1016).

Mr Kamlish: Finally, on the topic of your general experience in police contact with black victims and specifically race attacks. You have obviously been concerned enough about this over your time to make the points you have made in both of your statements?

A. Yes.

Q. It is not just a passing impression or a possibility. It is a clear impression you got from dealing with these cases over the years?

A. Yes, it is.

Q. You say it is not evidentially based, your view, but in terms of your empirical experience of these cases, it is in that sense you actually observe the police dealing differently in many cases with black victims of crime and victims of race attacks. You have observed it?

A. Yes, I have. Sometimes it is quite difficult to work out what it is that is different. It hinges on things like attitude and demeanour, on approach and manner, and those are often things that are quite difficult to extract (p.1027).

The embedded nature of this attitude of the police officers revealed by the nurse cannot begin to be challenged on the basis of cultural awareness training. It cannot even be challenged by imparting information and using rational arguments to 'prove' the truth. The subliminal racism can just be denied.

Another mechanism adopted by the police for denying the racist aspect of the murder hinges on the idea that people need to avoid criminal places and violence and keep areas distinct in race terms. If black boys go into white areas late at night they should accept that violence might occur. Inspector Bevan says that the murder was carried out by 'racist yobs' and that 'Stephen was in the wrong place at the wrong time'.

5. Colour blindness as justified by the 'impartiality' of the professional class

The discretion to act in a common-sense way in spite of policy directives from the top is a key aspect of police occupational culture. The resort to 'professionalism' or impartiality characterises the discourse at junior and middle ranking level. Several police officers at these levels use objectivity in their professional role to justify acting in a colour-blind way. Race makes no difference – 'a murder is a murder'. Denial is by resort to professionalism, liberalism or objectivity. This approach to gender and race blindness has been encouraged in wider society and is found to exist among many middle managers (Nkomo 1993).

Inspector Groves, for example, explains that colour is irrelevant to any investigation:

'Whether someone is black or white is totally irrelevant' (Inspector Groves p.1379)

'I do not differentiate at all.' (Detective Constable Pye p. 1737)

'Difficult to prove' (Detective Constable Tomlin p. 3031)

'Dealt with all victims in the same way' (Detective Constable Tomlin p. 3032).

'No matter what skin colour you are, a murder is a murder' (Detective Constable Budgen)

'I would say it was treated as any other murder at the time of the house to house.' (Detective Sergeant Kirkpatrick, who conducted house-to-house inquiries.)

'I did my job as a professional officer' (Detective Sergeant Crowley 4586)

'I am not racist because I am a liberal' (Detective Sergeant Cooper)

When we move up the police ranks we encounter a subtler way in which this professionalism is enacted and elaborated. Firstly, racism is trivialised. Take, for example, Inspector Little's remarks about his failure to discuss with the Lawrences whether the attack on Stephen was 'racist' (see above). Secondly, racism is ignored. When asked about the murder of Roland Adams, Detective Sergeant Crowley said he had not noticed in his investigating colleague's report that the gang had said: 'Get the nigger, get the nigger'. A critical piece of information which indicates the seriousness of the racist crime, and defines it as such, was effectively censored.

6. Denial as pleas of ignorance, errors and amnesia

Thinking differently from the norm leads to anxiety, according to Detective Chief Superintendent Barker:

> It is quite apparent that the two officers who first attended Well Hall Road later experienced post incident trauma, particularly when information about Stephen's background emerged as being a well motivated and hard working person (Day 38 p. 7474).

Officers were clearly surprised and shocked by the discovery that Stephen did not fit the assumed stereotype. This challenged the norm. Detective Chief Superintendent Barker, who carried out the review of the first investigation into Stephen's murder, did not question whether police officers could be racist. He did not even entertain the possibility (p.7474).

Sir Paul Condon assumed that some police officers admitted to colour blindness because they were worried about the challenges of their work. They played safe and thus made errors.

> I am privileged, I feel privileged to be in the presence of Mr & Mrs Lawrence again. The grief that they have felt I have personally shared, but for a group of officers I think who came — I am not defending what they said or how they behaved but I think when in such a challenging environment I think many of them took comfort in what they thought was safe territory. Safe territory is, say: I treat everyone the same, I am colour blind ... I think they, many of them, erred stupidly in not explaining their actions. (Paul Condon p.312)

Junior officers denied that there was any racism within the Metropolitan Police Force. Police Constable Smith said she had heard the 'odd tactless jokes' – but not by police officers. She could not recall what the jokes were or where she had heard them. Police Constable Clements said he had not heard any racist comments in the police force. Police Constable Gleason said he had not heard any racist jokes and could not remember police officers making racist remarks. Detective Inspector Bullock said he had never heard any racist jokes about black people but had heard some against the Irish, Scots and English. This is interesting when set alongside his use of the word coloured. Assistant Commissioner Johnston, who also used the word coloured, and apologised for doing so, saying he had not thought it offensive. Two senior officers did admit to racism in the police, but echoed the Commissioner's 'bad apple' theory – *'this is a minority, a small minority'* (Superintendent Mellish).

The direct versus the indirect style of questioning

The police constables and sergeants who were on the case soon after Stephen's murder were asked to comment on Doreen Lawrence's statement that police officers: *'did not want to dirty their hands with a black man's blood'*. In an atmosphere in which overt racism has effectively been outlawed in public discourse over the last twenty-five years, it is unlikely that anyone would reply in the affirmative in public. The nature of deep-seated fears about black people is that these are often repressed and unconscious. Asking police officers directly if they felt deep-seated racism is almost like asking if they were against justice and had no care for humanity. Denial would be inevitable.

7. The elite discourse of colour blindness – doing a good job

There were five transcripts of evidence where race, racism, racist, white, black, racial were not mentioned at all. Assistant Commissioner Nove does not mention race proactively. His denial/colour blindness is evident in his protestations that the police were now doing their job and were committed to doing it well. The implication is that could not therefore be racist. If race is not mentioned it cannot be an issue. This senior officer was put in charge of improving liaison with the family and with their solicitor Mr Khan, and took over in mid-994. The lawyer asks him how he went about improving communication with the Lawrences and he replies.

> **Q.** Were you able to communicate with them adequately?
>
> **A.** I think — this is a subjective judgment of me by myself — I think I managed to communicate in a way that was significantly enhanced above the way the Metropolitan Police had communicated with her before.
>
> **Q.** Why do you think that is the case?
>
> **A.** I don't know.
>
> **Q.** Your personality?

A. Well, I tried...

Q. I do not say that jokingly. It may be that you were the right person to deal with it?

A. I tried very hard. I really felt for them. I felt that somehow, some way, justice had to be delivered for them. I dealt honestly with every point they raised. If you look at these many minutes which I created of the meetings, they don't shrink from difficulty. Every time Mr or Mrs Lawrence or Mr. Khan made a complaint, I faithfully recorded it.

Q. Did it trouble you that they complained?

A. It did, in the sense that this was the first major investigation in all of my experience where there wasn't a reasonable relationship between the investigators and the victims or the relatives of the victims. This is a worst-case scenario. I cared about what we were doing. Ian Johnston cared about what we were doing. We really were trying to move this forward in imaginative ways. I have looked back through the minutes and collated in my mind the sort of things that Mr and Mrs Lawrence said to me and complained of. They were all about lost opportunities, particularly in the early days of the investigation. I couldn't impact that in any way. To come into an investigation 13 months on, an investigation which had been on a caretaking basis for some significant weeks, I understood, and to try to resurrect it in a meaningful way is very, very difficult indeed. But I did my best to communicate with Mr and Mrs Lawrence, and also with Mr Khan, in as good a way that I could.

Q. It is clear from the numerous records you have kept that you were not put off by what may sometimes have been difficult questions that were being asked and complaints?

A. Very difficult questions. I mean, there was no answer to: what if action had been taken earlier? (a) I couldn't turn the clock back; and (b) I didn't have a crystal ball which would tell me whether if, for instance, the arrests had taken place on the Saturday evening, whether, evidentially, the outcome would have been different. (p.8439 – 8440)

Assistant Commissioner Johnston also emphatically denies that there is racism in the police force. Here racism is explicitly addressed and the arguments used are designed to empathise with those who might make accusations of racism against the police, but his sincerity in denying racism is enough. No further explanation is given about his analysis, nor is it elicited.

Q. Mr Johnston, on this topic can I ask you finally and bluntly, so that we can see where the issues lie, how you react to the suggestion from your knowledge of this investigation, or these investigations: the suggestion that, if this had been a white middle class boy, the enquiry would have been different?

A. I genuinely don't believe that. I think it's widely recognised in the Metropolitan Police now, perhaps less so at the time of Stephen's death, the enormously damaging impact that a racist murder has, not only on the families of individuals concerned themselves but on the wider community, and I seriously don't believe the investigation then was any worse. I think it was, in terms of motivation, exactly the same as any other murder inquiry, and I hope that colleagues were able to convey some feeling about how they dealt with that. (p.8579)

His sincerity in denying racism occurs earlier in the evidence:

Q. I think I should ask you to address two issues that go beyond incompetence and the making of mistakes. You know it has long been suggested by the Lawrence family and by others that the investigation was tainted by racism?

A. Yes, sir.

Q. What, if any, views do you wish to express about that?

A. If the Lawrences feel that, that is very, very important; and it is for us to demonstrate that that is not the case. It is my firm belief that that is not the case. It is quite right that their concerns about it should be thoroughly and properly explored; and I can understand some of the analysis that leads them to that conclusion. I sincerely do not believe that to be the case, and I do hope that colleagues who have been here have left some impression of their views around this issue and the extent to which they were influenced or not by racist attitudes. (p.8570-8571)

8. Racism as something to do with black people out there – not in here

One Detective Constable expressed a characteristic form of racism that pervades social policy. He had not been on training courses because he didn't need to – for years he had learned about racism from: *'working in areas where there was a large black population'* (Detective Constable Tomlin p.3015).

Detective Constable Holden argued that she was able to understand how a black family might feel when their son had been killed in a racist attack because: *'from the age of 15 months old to the age of 17 I was actually brought up in Africa, so I do know and understand black people'* (p.3723). Clearly, she is viewing racism as something to do with understanding black people. Furthermore, she sees all black people as the same, including all the heterogeneous groups that live in the continent of Africa!

When senior officers use this idea of race as being to do with black people, the racism becomes increasingly obscure and difficult to challenge. Assistant Commissioner Johnston became involved in the murder case in 1994 when he had to apologise to the Lawrences for the failure of the investigations into Stephen's murder. In responding to questions, he says:

Q. You are aware of a recent Met report, ... which I understand is now to be published, although not previously, which shows on a wide study that black people were four times more likely to be stopped and searched in a street as white people; that is the broad finding?

A. Yes; and I think there are social democratic and other reasons for that; and if I can briefly elucidate, sir?

Q. Please.

A. If we look at the people who are likely to be out on the streets, youngsters who are truanting and excluded from schools, who are over-represented in the truanting statistics, enormously over-represented, and exclusion statistics, it is young black children. If you look at who else is out on the streets, it is the unemployed. If you look at the differential rates of unemployment, black people, for a range of reasons, some of which are understandable, some of which are abhorrent, are unemployed. If you look at police where police do their stop and search, it is in high crime areas. High crime areas tend to be areas of social deprivation. Who lives in areas of social deprivation? For a range of reasons, coloured people. So I wouldn't simply jump from the conclusion that because they were over-represented, that

that necessarily led to support for an allegation of racism. What I do agree with is that it is something that needs significant exploration and significant looking into, which was the whole basis of the setting up of that report. (p.8693-8694)

The Assistant Commissioner argues implicitly that racism is really nothing to do with the actions of the police force because it is expressed outside by society. Furthermore, racism by the police force prevents crime and prevents black people becoming more represented in the victim statistics.

In a slightly different slant on understanding 'black areas', more plausibly presented, Sir Paul Condon attributes racism to 'our cities', and expresses racism as social disadvantage, quoting from Lord Scarman's Report:

Racism is a feature throughout society. Racism is a feature in policing. I have always seen the challenge personally as being not to, for the police service, as Scarman said: "We do not set a social context. We do not create a social disadvantage. The problem lies in the social or economic conditions of many of our great cities". The challenge for policing is never to amplify those challenges. (Part II p.291)

This denial is arguably a key mechanism of racism in dominant discourse in the Press: *'Racism is usually elsewhere: in the past (during slavery or segregation) abroad (apartheid in South Africa), politically at the far right (racist parties) and socially at the bottom (poor inner cities, skinheads. This is true for both the conservative and liberal press'* (van Dijk 1993 p.182).

9. Racism conceived as cultural differences

Chapter 3 discussed the 'new racism' of cultural difference. Covert racism is linked to the idea of cultures other than white English as inferior. They are different from the norm. The shift to recognising difference has permeated the ranks of Senior Officers, some of whom mentioned difference as something to be aware of and work on. Their junior counterparts, on the other hand, are more likely to follow the discourse of colour blindness. A Superintendent who had a degree in Development Studies felt he wanted to acknowledge the idea of difference:

Q. Thank you. How do you feel about racial issues in the police force? What is your standpoint?

A. My standpoint is that difference is to be valued, that it is important that fair treatment is vital and I actually believe that people from different backgrounds whatever those might be, whatever criteria that you use, can only enrich and benefit society; and indeed the police service. And those are important issues and important issues for me. (McIvor, Day 6 p.973)

What this approach to difference means in practice for a murder investigation is not clear. McIvor states that racist crimes have implications for community harmony and the key difference would be that the crime is classified as racist. Cultural difference is equated with race.

Q. Have there been any difference in the investigation of those cases where race has been an issue?

A. They're classified differently which is because all racial incidents are specifically classified as such. But every effort is made to investigate every crime as expeditiously and thoroughly as possible.

Q. The difference in relation to a case that is classified as involving a question of race is simply the way in which it is recorded. Is that what you are saying?

A. I am saying they are classified differently. I am saying every incident is and should be investigated thoroughly. I have also said that racial incidents have other consequences that other crimes do not.

Q. The consequences which you refer to is not really a question of the investigation. You refer now to this question of effect upon the community, destabilising?

A. Community harmony, community stability, community well-being, yes.

Q. I see. Certainly there was nothing, as far as you are aware, that goes into an investigation itself, the offence or the crime being touched by race which is different from the investigation of another offence?

A. I think that is not a question that should be put to me as a uniformed officer. (p.959-960)

McIvor was one of the few officers analysed who publicly accepted that racism existed. Yet when the issue of police responsibility for incorporating the idea of racism into their investigation is raised, he ends up by conveying doubt about its usefulness for the police force; understanding racism was useful merely to prevent community tension.

Racism is once again positioned out there. The purpose of recording racist incidents then becomes a way not of monitoring and examining the organisation's responses, but of merely record-keeping for public and government, so that action can be seen in the business of monitoring. Racism continues to be viewed as being out there in the community. Monitoring is a part of public relations.

Also clear from the proceedings is how senior officers often see training to combat racism as being about cultural difference:

> So, I think what we are saying is that we recognise the limitations of the training over the last few years. It is a position, which is broadly comparable to training elsewhere in the UK. We recognise its limitations. We are trying to reposition ourselves. We have an excellent programme which has, for example, little scenarios where there are tests of individuals' reactions: so, Ethiopian running away, called by a police officer; he does not think the police officer is calling him, because this sort of movement in his own country is only directed at a child; the officer thinks he is ignoring him, shouts at him; he then thinks: 'This guy is being very, very rude to me'; the police officer waves his hand, and the waving of his hands in his own country is only used for animals. There are these types of scenarios painted out, to try and get through the much more subtle forms of what is clearly offensive behaviour to people of other races. These are, in a sense, in the rough and tough everyday life of policing, fairly sophisticated messages to put through. They are very important messages, very worthwhile messages, and messages that we are determined will get through. (Assistant Commissioner Johnston:)

Sir Paul Condon talks about diversity when making reference to new approaches to training. In his remarks quoted below, it appears that not even cultural differences are important. His whole approach has become individualised and racism is no longer a consideration. It has disappeared:

We have developed new training to address the challenges of diversity. I am not just treating people fairly, but treating them as individuals. Had officers at various stages responded to the needs, if I may, of Mr and Mrs Lawrence, of Duwayne Brooks in ways that reflected them as individuals, their anxieties, their needs, their concerns, their pain, then I think rather than when faced with challenge – just falling back on 'we treat everyone the same' — then I think different things would have happened and I think we recognise and have built upon the training.

In an ideal world, we would indeed want to get beyond race, but this cannot begin to happen until racial stereotyping and racism are acknowledged and the power behind interactions based upon stereotyping and racism recognised.

10. Racism conceived as a one-way black/white duality

When racism is admitted, the white/black duality is taken on board uncritically. Superintendent McIvor, who was the most senior police officer on duty the night of Stephen's murder, told the Inquiry how he would classify a racist attack if white youth/s had attacked a black youth/s.

> **Q.** I mean, an attack by white youths on a black youth by itself would not necessarily mean it was a racist attack, would it?
>
> **A.** Well, I mean, I would always classify it as such. I mean, I would.
>
> **Q.** Whatever the motive?
>
> **A.** I think I would classify it as such certainly at the outset. I mean the circumstances – it would be foolish not to in my view.
>
> **Q.** Would you not also want to know whether it was something that was combined with, say, an attempt at robbery, or out of some kind of jealousy over a shared lover or a revenge attack for something that had been done?
>
> **A.** Yes, I would in due course but, I have to say, right at that time my recollection of the information was that a group of white youths had killed a black person in the street and for me it would be certainly – it would be disingenuous to think that that was at that time anything other than a racial attack. Certainly the perception and often it is perceptions that we are dealing with, would have been that it was a racial attack.

Q. Yes?

A. And community perceptions, you know, are important, indeed vital. (p.963-964)

It is assumed here that racism is only about black/white and operates along a one-way continuum. The Superintendent admits that he records this as a racist incident because it can play an important role in defusing tensions in the area to be policed.

A further assumption is apparent: racism is about a straightforward division between black and white. For example, Mr Gompertz asked at least two police officers who denied police racism whether they had black friends. Here racism is assumed to be about the separation of races and about apartheid in social relations based on hatred.

The fact that the family liaison officer to the Lawrences was white was regarded as critical. The lawyers suggested that the police needed to be sensitive to the needs of a black family. These suggestions influenced the interpretation in the Inquiry report, which argued that a different approach might be required for black families because of *cultural* differences.

> Plainly Mr and Mrs Lawrence were not dealt with or treated as they should have been. Their reaction and their attitude after their son's murder were those of a grieving family. The fact that they were in their eyes and to their perception patronised and inappropriately treated exhibits plain but unintentional failure to treat them appropriately and professionally within their own culture and as a black grieving family (The Stephen Lawrence Inquiry 1999: 185).

11. Racism conceived as essentialising

Like many others in the Inquiry, Inspector Bevan uses the idea of racism as a fixed and singular phenomenon. It is in people's minds. In his denial he says that he did not know the murder was racist because a white youth could just as well have been murdered and '*we do not know what went through the assailants' minds, possibly we will never know*' (p.3623). This line is echoed by Detective Constable Holden who, in her answers about her role as family liaison officer, spends a great deal of time denying racism.

Q. What was your view as to the motive for Stephen being killed at the time you were acting as family liaison officer?

A. I was obviously aware that it was a racist murder, but what the motive was I couldn't say.

Q. Is not racism a motive?

A. It was, but on the night I wasn't there, so I couldn't say what their motive was for killing him. I really can't say.

Q. A motive is racism?

A. Yes, that's right.

Q. Stephen was killed by a bunch of sadistic racists. Do you not accept that?

A. I do, but I can't say what was in their minds at the time.

Q. Do you not accept he was killed because he was black?

A. I really can't answer that. (p.3803)

Also evident in Holden's remarks is the conflation of racism and racialism. She cannot accept or fails to understand the context of a murder which is racist and which has implications for power between groups based on notions of superiority and inferiority.

Conclusions

This analysis of racism talk illustrates and illuminates the ways in which racism is reproduced and maintained in wider society. The masking of racism in dominant discourse has made invisible the wide variety of forms that racism takes. Managerial and professional racism is masked by dominant discourse that highlights cultural difference, or projects racism onto some white working class estates, or as residing solely in the inner cities.

The focus of this chapter has been on unmasking the invisible racism within organisations, notably the racism as expressed by senior and junior officers in the police force. The managerial and professional racism within a specific culture needs to be uncovered and unpacked. If its various forms are not understood, intervention will not be linked to the analysis of the problem. Awareness about racism as removed from everyday discourse is impossible and so cannot be effective.

Police discourse about racism in the Metropolitan Police is based on denial. This denial is expressed in different ways. For some officers (across the hierarchy) there is an absence of discourse on race. These officers do not even mention the words race, racial racist, black or white in their evidence. Those who discuss racism openly, almost unfailingly deny it. Denial may be in the form of a meritocratic colour-blind approach which says that everyone is treated the same. Senior officers' denials may resort to positive self-presentation; a cry about sincerity; or a notion that racism exists only in the inner cities or amongst black communities – here the euphemism for racism is 'social disadvantage'. Within the Metropolitan Police Force, the minority who did accept the existence of racism within their force argued it lay with a small number of bad individuals or that it was about a misunderstanding about cultural differences.

This culture of denial is deeply rooted in and legitimated at the highest levels by the Metropolitan Police. It was argued in Chapter 3 that the occupational culture of the police allows a discretionary power to junior police officers. This discretionary power, manifest in the officers' behaviour, is the discretion to express different discourses of racism. The denial of racism by senior officers draws a boundary around a white male exclusionary culture. This culture is then perceived as the norm. Racism is made visible in police discourse by reference to black people having special treatment or a view that racism belongs somewhere 'out there'. These views legitimate whiteness as a norm.

Educative intervention in this culture has to be transforming and long-term. Training courses aimed at taking a few middle and junior-ranking officers towards enlightenment about racism cannot hope to impact on the nature and form of racism in this occupational culture. The culture of discretionary power at the lowest levels of the police force legitimates the practice of racism. Any educational or long-term intervention has to grapple with this situation. A greater transparency in how communities are policed and how police officers conduct their everyday interactions with members of the public (i.e.

an independent scrutinising authority), together with greater public accountability, will do more to challenge racism than all the short training courses in valuing cultural diversity or on combating racism could ever hope to achieve.

5
Training to Combat Racism
– past and present

Introduction

Over the last fifteen to twenty years millions of pounds have been spent on training to combat racism. Most of this training has taken place in individual work organisations. There is an army of trainers who deliver this training across differing work organisations and occupational groups. In the past very little of this training has been evaluated. Some studies in the USA have questioned the competence of trainers. A recent poll suggested 50% of 'diversity' trainers did not know what they were doing (Ellis and Sonnenfield 1994). The evidence from the Stephen Lawrence Inquiry suggests that training for the police on combating racism was a disaster. Many police officers either could not remember their training or did not see the need for it.

This chapter explores the history and development of training to combat racism in Britain and the current situation and limitations. The author has had detailed discussions with training providers and has carried out a review of material in the CRE's library (see Appendix One). This helps to highlight some of the current problems associated with training to combat racism in the UK.

Historical context

Concomitant training and educational approaches have developed alongside social policy. The four main social policy approaches are concerned with stressing and encouraging assimilation; pluralistic integration; legislative action on racial discrimination and challenging racism as part of a wider process of cultural change. All these social policy emphases have had concomitant training/educational approaches associated with them. At each stage of the development of campaigns on education and training, antiracist campaigning by parents and activists, as well as research into discrimination has profoundly affected the way social policy developed.

Assimilation and integration

In the 1950s and 1960s, the emphasis was on assimilation. This involved teaching immigrants to adapt to the UK and to learn English. Government, as a way of institutionalising this policy in education, began bussing black children away from their local areas into a variety of schools. Bussing was resisted and there were parental campaigns to put an end to it. For adults, training programmes were developed on English for Immigrants. These programmes, some developed by the Industrial Language Training Centres, included developing an understanding of 'culture' so that learning through experience and understanding the 'other' could be more fruitful.

These initiatives were closely followed by the concept of integration. One way to foster good race relations was to learn about 'other' cultures and ensure all children learned about them too. In 1966 Roy Jenkins defined this approach as: '*equal opportunity accompanied by cultural diversity in an atmosphere of mutual tolerance*'. Multicultural policies were debated and implemented. But this equal opportunity was interpreted in many institutions as a focus on African Caribbean and South Asian cultures. There followed training programmes on 'black cultures', including issues such as religion, dress and food. However, white cultures were never examined; they were left invisible. Culture came to mean black cultures and implicit in learning about these cultures was the idea that they were different from the norm – they were inferior in comparison to white British cultures. Culture became linked to ideas of race and racism and racism was masked by reference to culture.

The implementation of equal opportunities in the context of cultural pluralism was undermined by a series of Immigration Acts designed to keep black people out of Britain. Good race relations was inextricably linked to keeping the numbers of immigrants low. If numbers rose too high, went the argument, race relations would suffer. Black people were repeatedly seen as unwelcome, not as part of Britain; restrictions on their entry would lead to better social or race relations. The 1968 and 1971 Acts strengthened institutional racism in immigration control. The 1981 Nationality Act established citizenship based on patriality, i.e. those whose parents or grand-parents had been born in Britain. The 1988 Immigration Act made residents in Britain prove they could maintain their relatives here without recourse to public funds, thus implying that black people were a burden on the Welfare State. Harmonisation of stricter im-migration and asylum controls in Europe led to the 1993 Asylum and Immigration Appeals Act, under which visitors lost the right of appeal against entry (Bhavnani 1994).

At the same time, there was criticism of policies of multiculturalism – from both the left and the right. The left argued that understanding the 'other' or black cultures did not tackle the power relations of racism. This 'saris, steel bands and samosas' approach led to an exoticisation of black cultures, which left the white culture un-explored and untouched. The right argued that it was important to keep 'cultures' distinct and campaigned for this. Many different arguments were used to argue for keeping 'cultures' or religions distinct and so-called 'authentic' (Sahgal and Yuval-Davis 1992).

Islamic fundamentalism highlighted the problems of Western secular societies. Fundamentalists viewed the West as blasphemous, non-respectful, racist and promiscuous. Their views were fuelled by an experience of racism in Britain and elsewhere, and a prevalent dominant discourse that Islam was backward. The Runnymede Trust recognised the specificity of anti-Muslim racism by setting up a Commission on Islamophobia.

'Common sense' arguments for black people to adapt to 'British traditions' came from people such as Ray Honeyford, a headmaster of a middle school in Bradford, later dismissed because of his racism (Honeyford 1984; 1988). Writing in the *Salisbury Review*, a journal of 'conservative thought', Honeyford argued the failure of 'West Indians' by the school system was not because of racism but was a consequence of their 'cultural problems'.

The roots of black educational failure are in reality located in the West Indian family structure and values, and in the work of misguided radical teachers whose motives are basically political'. (Honeyford 1984 p. 31 quoted in Troyna and Williams 1986 p. 96)

Legislation and antiracist initiatives

These arguments for cultural distinctiveness and separation were counterpointed by policies on race equality and antiracism. The policies on race equality were given momentum by the disquiet of black parents in the 1960s and early 1970s over the institutionalised inequality in the education system. The disproportionate numbers of African Caribbean children designated educationally sub-normal (ESN) was to lead to parents' campaigns, spearheaded by Bernard Coard's book (1971) *How the West Indian Child is made Educationally Subnormal by the British School System.* The book sold over 10,000 copies, adding to pressure for change. After years of campaigning, Shirley Williams, then Secretary of State for Education, set up the Committee of Inquiry into the Education of the Children from Ethnic Minority Groups, chaired by Sir Anthony Rampton. The Rampton Report (1981) identified intentional and unintentional racism in the education system and recognised it as a key factor in disadvantaging black children.

The 1976 Race Relations Act moved work organisations to implement equal opportunity policies. In 1980, the Scarman Report on the Brixton disorders pushed the drive for making race equality and antiracism visible and explicit in policy development in local government. Resistance to multiculturalism increased in light of the emerging evidence about the prevalence of racism. The Greater London Council (GLC), along with other left-wing Councils, generated a wealth of antiracist initiatives, which they saw as a more appropriate policy response than multiculturalism. Local government policy shifted. It moved to educating white individuals about their personal attitudes through racism awareness training. The programmes were aimed at making the links between power and prejudice. An army of race awareness trainers was employed to run generic programmes in local government.

The decline of race awareness training

In the late 1980s much of this activity diminished for a variety of reasons: cutbacks in local government; a decline in and frustration with the work of race units; a Thatcherite backlash against political correctness (Cohen 1999); critiques of RAT from the left, notably by Sivanandan, and the crudity of implementation of Equal Opportunity/antiracist policies and related training (Gurnah 1984; Sivanandan 1985).

The relative silence on training

The complicated nature of institutional racism, left undissected at the time, did not allow for a range of social policy responses or training approaches that took account of the changing natures of racisms, identities, cultures and their overlaps. There is a taboo on discussing such issues: uncertainty and confusion partly explains the silence we experience today. Because analysis of the nature of racism was crude, it generated crude practical responses and antiracist initiatives declined. Such crude responses to racism were particularly critiqued in the report into the murder of Ahmed Iqbal Ullah at Burnage High School in Manchester (Macdonald Report 1989).

Antiracism versus multiculturalism

The contest between antiracism and multiculturalism continues. The problem with both approaches is that both can 'essentialise' or fix ideas about certain groups forever. They have failed to take into consideration the notions of both racism and ethnicity as imagined, fluid and affected by particular historical and political contexts. Furthermore, both approaches positioned people as victims, whereas individuals and groups make and re-make their own identities and are not empty vessels into which their ancestral origin is placed forever, removed from other societal influences (Mac an Ghail 1999; Cohen 1999; Hall 1992; Gilroy 1987).

This polarisation of antiracism and multiculturalism represents a false dichotomy. In some senses their supporters are on the same side, arguing for some fixedness of race (colour) or culture.

Types of training to combat racism

A recent review of training to combat racism has categorised the approaches to training in five areas, itemised below. The features under each heading have been taken from a single source or multiple sources; the literature in this area is not coherent or extensively analysed. I have tried my best to present all the information I have been able to find. Under each heading, there may follow both principles of the training and its genesis, or just the principles. The five categories are:

- Race Information Training
- Race Awareness Training
- Race Equality Training
- Antiracism training
- Educational approach (Luthra and Oakley 1991).

This author has added two more categories: Cultural Awareness Training and Diversity Training. These approaches each have key features, summarised below. There are considerable overlaps between the approaches and they are not as distinct as they may at first appear.

Race Information Training

- is based on the premise that white people are unaware of racial discrimination and its effects

- aims to give information and thus targets the cognitive level

- is imparted primarily in lecture format by race relations experts

- aims to give information about black ethnicities – food, religion, dress etc.

- Effectiveness depends on receptivity of trainee

Race Awareness Training

- was endorsed by the Government and implemented by local government – it was seen as an important step in tackling both institutional and individual racism

- developed in full after the rebellions of the early 1980s and the Scarman Report

- it is practically based, in the hope of leading to action – aimed primarily at middle class managers and professionals

- it defines racism as a white problem because it was socialised into white people and institutions

- it is facilitated by encouraging personal ownership of racism and styles of facilitation – often extremely challenging and/or confrontational for trainees

- it encouraged a moral stance, which stressed the nastiness and immorality of racism (Luthra and Oakley 1991; Macdonald Inquiry 1989; Gurnah 1984).

Race Equality Training

- stresses the legal obligation to practice race equality

- is often part of a wider organisational strategy which stresses equal opportunity goals

- stresses change in behaviour at work/in a professional role – does not consider personal attitudes relevant

- places more emphasis on likely occurrence of racial discrimination rather than analysis of causes

- presents three stages of training – selling or conversion stage to senior managers; planning exercises to develop strategy; skills development for practitioners to develop policy and procedures fairly and with discretion (Luthra and Oakley 1991).

Antiracism Training

- responds to the limitations of the earlier approaches of race awareness and race equality training

- argues that racism is not about personal attitudes, nor only about knowledge of discriminatory behaviour but is about part of a wider organisational strategy to achieve cultural and organisational change

- emphasises both attitudinal and behavioural change – the approach may consist of lectures, discussions, collaborative exercises – it is not judgmental

- provides specially targeted independent training

- is confined to a few authorities and voluntary organisations up to late 80s

Cultural awareness training

- gives information about black cultures in terms of food, religion, dress, language etc. For example, training aimed at prison officers has handouts, which explain details about religions, dress and food (see CRE 1989 *Racial Equality and the Prison Service: the case for training*).

- develops an approach which encourages participants to become aware of differences between cultures by examining interactions between different ethnic groups, such as making eye contact, asking questions.

- can be both didactic and experience led, with use of videos – cross cultural communication which was in vogue in the 1980s, was developed by BBC Education into a video for educational use entitled 'Cross-Cultural Communication'

Diversity Training

- began in the USA and aimed to 'set a new mood', moving away from affirmative action as a social justice idea to managing diversity

- is based on a business case for equal opportunities: an argument that organisations can compete more effectively for skilled labour by drawing on employees from an array of cultural backgrounds – a 'question of business survival' (Ellis and Sonnenfield 1994)

- argues that prejudice and conflict and miscommunication inhibit productivity, influence turnover and affect the financial performance of the firm

- considers virtually all the ways in which people differ, not just the more obvious issues of gender, ethnicity and disability

- is not focused on positive action; aims to have an impact on organisational culture, flexibility, team effectiveness (Kandola 1995).

Educational approaches

- include content on personal development – some argue this is critical for ownership and action on change;

- are postulated on a belief that if training is forced upon individuals, it is less likely to bring about change;

- are longer term, stressing personal development through discussion, personal reflection and information giving

- stress attitudes and knowledge

- offer a general model of personal development in which race-specific training/education forms part of the content

- are seen as non-directive and claim no clear standardised outcomes.

From the early 1990s

In the last few years, approaches to racism and training concerning it have appeared in a less homogeneous form. Training is piecemeal, fragmented, rationally based, short, and developed for specific audiences. There has also been a decline in provision, probably related to budget cuts. Training to combat racism is being developed for particular target groups, such as human resource managers, policy staff, those in the voluntary sector, young white people, black managers and so on. Its content and approach is also more likely to vary for different groups. It may come in the form of: paper information regarding new developments in legislation; outside speakers at seminars to reinforce a policy direction; or a short course which aids planning and policy development. Training to combat racism in the 1990s has been influenced by all the approaches outlined above. Older and newer approaches are to be found in the same course content. Often they may not be 'new'. Much training focus has been put into management development. Mainstreaming equalities into management development has been much discussed but it is too early to assess what the impact of this might be.

The author has examined local authority committee reports written in response to the Stephen Lawrence Inquiry and had discussions with local authority staff and co-ordinating organisations for local government. These information sources suggest a mix of provision has developed in training, which may be characterised as:

General Equalities training

There are general courses of training on equalities, which include learning about elements of race discrimination, as well as other discriminations. Content includes compliance with anti-discrimination law and Best Value legislation. It may contain elements of race equality training as outlined above. Related to a general equalities training is *anti-harassment training* for middle and senior managers to ensure compliance with the law. Some local authorities have put these initiatives in place in response to growing numbers of grievance cases being taken out by black employees in local government (GLEA 2000). General anti-harassment training exists which includes racial harassment in the course content. Courses are short and concerned with legislation, and they offer case studies of how to prevent harassment arising. Wider short courses in this area are likely to be called 'anti-discriminatory practices' and would be run on equality legislation. Courses run for managers emphasise a task-focused approach to *developing indicators and reviewing services*, rather than a personalised awareness-raising approach. This may become increasingly important given the legislation on best value. There do not appear to be any independent evaluations of the effects of this training.

Courses have also emerged in *managing or valuing diversity* in central government, much influenced by Pearn Kandola's work (1995; 1997). Managing or valuing diversity began in the USA, and aimed to 'set a new mood', shifting from affirmative action as a social justice idea to managing diversity, based on a business case for equal opportunities. These courses may include some specific work on race discrimination, but stress the way managers must work with their staff to build team effectiveness by encouraging a diversity of opinions; they must beware of stereotyping. The recognition of the benefits of diversity has developed in tandem with the business case for equal opportunities and a stress on individual rather than group differences in organisations. It explores virtually all the ways in which people differ, not just the more obvious categories of gender, ethnicity and disability, arguing that each individual must be developed and may need differing approaches. It is not focused on positive action, but aims to have an impact on organisational culture, flexibility and team effectiveness. The logic of these approaches suggests an individualised approach to difference, based on new models of human resource management (Kandola 1995). The model of diversity management developed by Pearn Kandola is in vogue and increasingly used in central government but has yet to be widely adopted in local government.

Specific training on combating racism

More specific training to address racism is piecemeal and fragmented. A range of differing groups is targeted to receive training of this kind. There may be isolated initiatives on '*cultural awareness*' aimed at front-line staff – in other words, information about religion, languages, food of differing minority ethnic groups in the area.

A series of events and seminars have been initiated in rural areas, where there are smaller numbers of black people compared with the inner cities. Recent initiatives include LARRIE (Local Authority Race Relations Information Exchange) workshops and responses by the Further Education Unit (1988) to invitations to work in primarily white areas. These may consist of half or one-day workshops to develop policy, examine relevant legislation and exchange ideas of contacts and practice. These courses focus on race equality, rather than culture.

There are pockets of work in education and in youth work specifically with white groups. For example, there have been initiatives designed to focus on antiracist work in all-white schools (Children's Society 1999) and in youth work in mainly white areas, such as Devon (Fusion Devon Project, Dhalech 1999). A series of activities have been developed aimed at young white working class men in inner cities. Some of these have involved action research and have been of a longer-term nature. The few that have been written up include Hewitt (1996); Dadzie (1997); Camden Race Equality Council (2000).

Training aimed at ethnic minorities

The setting by the Home Secretary of targets for the representation of ethnic minorities in the Police, Fire and Probation Services has led to concerted efforts to push *positive action initiatives aimed at black staff*. There are programmes planned for black managers, mentoring schemes, black networks in the Civil Service and other similar initiatives, aimed primarily at black and ethnic minority staff. These make little impact on the overall culture of the organisation. Managers continue to remain either colour-blind or defensive (Bhavnani and Coyle 2000). One of the difficulties this approach presents is that black and ethnic minority staff grow in self-esteem and aim for senior positions, only to be frustrated by not being appointed.

Teaching aims and manuals aimed at improving professional practice

The author reviewed training packs and manuals collected at the CRE library. These reveal certain limitations, which are discussed below in more detail. The approaches to training aim variously to

- change personal attitudes

- change professional behaviour

- provide knowledge about cultures, religions, languages etc., and/or histories of black peoples.

Certain of the publications include all these elements. Some target audiences such as police, teachers and social workers have had training developed for them. Many training packs are specifically targeted but have general use. The training has frequently been developed along the lines of specific modules or short courses (ranging from one to several days) on racism or valuing cultures. (See Appendix I for lists of resources examined at the CRE library.)

There have also been attempts to incorporate awareness raising in professional manuals for social workers, youth workers, housing officials, police officers and prison officers. These modules are fairly similar, although with slightly different emphases in approach and content. They date from the mid to late 1980s. The issues emphasised in these packs concern

- the appreciation of cultural differences (ethnically sensitive social work for example)

- challenging stereotypes

- understanding legislation

- recruitment of and partnership with black people in tackling racism.

For social workers who work with the elderly, there is a focus on black elderly and their needs. These publications date from the 1980s and aim to increase knowledge as well as change the behaviour of white professionals towards black people. They incorporate elements of the six approaches outlined above (excluding diversity training).

Effectiveness of training approaches

The analysis of current training provision and information highlights some of the deficiencies of current training to combat racism in the UK. Firstly, *training aims are not consistent*. Courses vary in content from imparting knowledge about the law to having a discussion with a 'leader' from a local community organisation. Participants may have to work through a pack of training materials which cover issues such as stereotyping, histories, what racism is, to more narrowly based content such as racism in the workplace (see for example, Brown 1999).

At the level of design of *content and approach*, further problems arise. For example, if the training is about imparting knowledge about slavery, for instance, or a particular religion, it is based on an assumption that racism is about ignorance. If training is based on emotive feelings, it has an experiential element and is defined by individualised actions. If it focuses on policy and procedures, it is about monitoring and changing bureaucratic systems. Should training be about individual or institutional change or both? What is the content of a course on institutionalised racism? Should it be about the history and roots of racism? Is it about taking moral stances? Is it to comply with legislation? Is it to put the business case for tackling racial discrimination? These debates have not been resolved, neither are they adequately linked together.

Different *teaching approaches* fuel this confusion. Many courses are based on the premise that contact with members of different ethnic groups, or promoting the benefits of diversity or race equality will clear up misconceptions (Ellis and Sonnenfield 1994). Should approaches be based on encouraging greater self-awareness or on being punitive about racism? Methods have ranged from the didactic to the confrontational. A good categorisation of methods is given in Dadzie (1999) [Appendix II]. It may be that these various approaches to content and approach are all appropriate in different contexts – that it is not a case of either/or but that a mixture of approaches may be necessary depending on the context.

Significantly, training is *isolated* from 'in there' and it is off the shelf. It is packaged, categorised and delivered. It is separated out and rarely integrated into other sorts of learning. There is very little emphasis on anyone but the 'other'. There is frequently no focus on the participants themselves and their identities, colour, religion, loyalty and so on. There is no consideration of the participants' discretionary, professional or managerial power to practise racism. Training rarely focuses on the invisible racism of government discourse or the media, nor on the denial of racism by senior policy makers and managers.

No explicit attention is given to gender or sexuality, or to the specificity of racisms – in other words, racialised social relations – in any of the packs that were evaluated. Furthermore, they show no evidence of collaborative work requiring everyone to own the issues and pursue wide-ranging discussions over a period of time. The assumptions about black versus white pervade many packs. However, there has been some interesting work on identity in a recent Commission for Racial Equality pack (*Open Talk, Open Minds* 1991). This *encourages* young people to be aware of their own cultural background, identities and travels, while also stressing commonalties. A pack was recently developed by Stella Dadzie for the Camden Race Equality Council (2000) in response to the attack on Richard Everett, in which young people were involved in developing a resource about racism to be used with teachers, youth workers and others.

The modules and courses on cultural awareness are also beset with problems. Take the police training courses as an example. Are they about educating police officers about the 'community' (ill defined and vague)? Or are they about bettering race relations outside the police force? The content of courses frequently fails to address the sexist and racist canteen culture. A programme for police training entitled Community and Race Relations Training has been condemned as such a failure (Holdaway 2000; Stephen Lawrence Inquiry 1999) that junior police officers have forgotten anything they learned and feel 'everyone should be treated the same' (Stephen Lawrence Inquiry 1999). A culture of sexism and racism exists in the occupational police culture. No action is taken and on the rare occasions it is, police officers feel unable to speak freely (Nottinghamshire Police 1999). Furthermore, the emphasis in police training programmes has been about understanding different cultures, so may well detract from 'the conflicts of race relations in which the police can be involved' (Holdaway 2000 p.5).

The local context in which training is delivered is rarely acknowledged as a key part of the training work. One recently developed training module in Tower Hamlets (1998), called the Headstart Module, is aimed at young people in schools. It has information about Tower Hamlets and concerns identity. It explores power through quizzes and has exercises on myths about race. However, the module fails to include white antiracists in its photographs on combating racism and gives no information about how the content was developed.

Training courses are rarely independently evaluated. The report titled *Winning the Race* saw training to combat racism as a failure (HMIC 1999). Because of its essentially didactic nature, the use of knowledge-based learning, such as a lecture, appears to have little effect in encouraging the ownership or recognition of racism, unless there is prior commitment or receptivity by trainees to the information.

Evaluations of the effectiveness of racism awareness training in the US suggest that the confrontational 'forced' approach leads to resistance to acknowledging racism or else engenders a crusading approach, neither of which appears to have any effect on organisational or professional work (Luthra and Oakley 1991). Simply pointing out differences between groups can also increase hostility and misunderstanding and imply that one group is inferior to another (Hewstone and Brown 1986). New stereotypes may be created and resentment aroused as a result of poorly executed courses. It has been argued that one-shot contact situations do not work, and that training must take place carefully over time (Ellis and Sonnenfield 1994).

Over the last fifteen years, there has been growing reluctance to talk about racism. This reluctance is due to a number of factors. We have been witness to colour blindness in dominant discourse until the Stephen Lawrence Inquiry. Under the Thatcher administration initiatives on discrimination or disadvantage were deracialised. The legacy of local government initiatives and 1980s identity politics, together with race awareness training, induced guilt, making people feel uncomfortable to discuss issues concerning racism openly. The rise of 'diversity' as a catch-all term, which offends no one, needs to be seen in this light. The taboo on speaking about race can have negative effects; race is all around us, but never openly spoken about (Bhavnani and Foot 2000). Even the willingness to discuss it vanishes once organisations realise that *people do find the subject matter uncomfortable and worry about political correctness, so we have to show clients it's about competitive advantage'* (Vernon 1999).

The present author identifies the following problems with the materials reviewed:

- There are few signs of an 'educational' longer term approach, partly because of lack of resources but also related to seeing racism as something 'out there'

- Too little attention is paid to the specific context of racism i.e. what types of culture does an organisation have, in what types of housing and neighbourhood is racism expressed, what type of collusion or challenge to racism exists through discourse and so on

- There is insufficient emphasis on white ethnicities and identities alongside black, and insufficient attention to national identities

- There is little work which acknowledges the embedding of racism in other social relations such as class, age, gender, sexuality

- Connections are seldom made to wider social and economic processes. These would help participants understand their own position better and see how racism manifests itself not only locally in interactions between local residents, but also in the media, police, government, local government

- Few of the materials indicate that everyone should be involved in challenging racism, rather than just a few black people and white activists. The message given is that ownership of tackling racism lies in just a few hands.

Understanding the limitations of current race training

Colour Blindness in the mainstream

The government, press and media have legitimated a colour-blind approach. Race in the 1990s became neutralised. No process or dialogue was initiated on how racism could be challenged. Racism had disappeared from public consciousness or was merely included in a general equalities agenda. Until the Stephen Lawrence Inquiry, racism was rarely explicitly mentioned as an urgent matter for public policy. Agenda on social policy and planning has become a reaction to a specific event – currently the Lawrence Inquiry. The neutralisation of debate can make managers feel defensive about managing black staff for fear of being accused of racism (Holdaway 2000; GLEA 2000). There is hesitancy and lack of confidence about openly discussing racism, as if it were a not legitimate issue

(Bhavnani and Foot 2000). This gender and colour blindness arising from social policy discourse is then considered the norm in organisations (Nkomo 1992), and to speak about it is seen as inappropriate.

Conceptions of racism

Racism has changed and shifted, as differences in emphases in social policy illustrate. There has been confusion about race, ethnicity and culture. Training has generally focused narrowly on white versus black, with the microscope on the 'black' need for positive intervention. Where this was not the case, as with racism awareness training, the outcome was a focus on individual white people, who were made to feel guilty and thus immobilised (Sivanandan 1985).

More recently, there has been a growing assumption that racism defines overt racism only, thus rendering other racisms invisible. The five young men accused of Stephen's murder were held up as an example of the 'evils' or 'disease' of overt racism. This kind of racism is far easier to identify and for the media to deal with. Macpherson drew attention to covert racism. Senior managers in organisations could be part of the 'unwitting' procedures or the 'collective failure' which characterises institutional racism. Such racisms seem miles apart. The one is tangible, apparently open to 'real evidence'; the other is open to debate about its existence. The relationship between these racisms appears non-existent, yet one legitimates the other (see Chapter 4).

Black-white dualism

Much training on racism in the past has assumed a fairly consistent separation between black and white (ethnic minority is coded for black – or communities of colour). Two issues make this separation problematic. Firstly, only one half of the issue has been subject to intense scrutiny – blackness. In other words, skin colour and black cultures are in the spotlight, whereas white ethnicities are not examined or monitored.

Secondly, there is an assumption that black and white are each homogeneous; this then influences social policy. Similarities across class and/or gender and/or race do not get examined. The overlapping of identities and their changing nature according to context and history are critical to the design and targeting of education and training programmes. Although race equality training followed race awareness training, emphasising the relation of race equality strategies to overall strategies, it is difficult to assess their impact in practice. It is not yet understood that the acknowledgement of heterogeneous plural communities, varying in power between and within themselves, has to be a basic feature of effective training.

Senior policy makers and managers

There is little training aimed at middle and senior managers that is designed to be proactively preventative of racism. When short courses are run, they are frequently related to concerns about employment tribunal cases in local authorities, and/or the increasing numbers of grievance and tribunal cases being brought by individuals on race discrimination grounds (GLEA 1998). Or courses are set up in response to a racist attack or murder.

Training for senior managers is becoming more problem-focused rather than being part of any change management initiatives or a response to cultural change. It is becoming generalised under an equalities label. It is unspecific about the different social relations of inequality, such as disability, age, sexuality. There is a movement to develop a generic standard for equalities for local government and this will influence the type of training managers receive.

The issue of class is not considered within equalities. Policy on social exclusion which covers the poor (unemployed, homeless, etc.) is separated from equalities work, although mention is made of different groups who may experience social exclusion in different ways, such as teenage girls, African Caribbean origin boys. The effects of these approaches are that many authorities use the term 'disadvantage'; equality issues are thus problematised, inequality is viewed separately and out of context from the lived experience of daily life. Initiatives that take account of overlapping inequalities and assess how to improve actions based on that understanding are virtually non-existent.

Managers still have poor levels of awareness about how to manage black staff, and fail to handle underperformance or other productivity issues that may arise competently. The problem is left to fester or else the managers resort to using the formal processes of discipline immediately, to forestall accusations of racism (GLEA 1998). There is much discomfort over issues of race as the numbers of such incidents rise and the failure of managers to act on race equality persists (Hunt and Palmer 1999).

Conclusions

Training to combat racism has failed. Piecemeal attempts at intervention in the late 1990s appear to be repeating the same old mistakes. This has happened because the social policy initiatives which influenced training courses were misconceived because of the failure to unravel racism. These misconceptions have had the following consequences in training:

- Racism appears to be defined as something to do with cultures of black people

- Whiteness has been invisible since the late 1980s and the days of racism awareness training

- Training to combat racism has been marginalised. It is not embedded in everyday social relations – racism is seen as 'something out there' which has little to do with 'us'

- There has thus been confusion about content and approach.

- Training content has appeared in the form of imparting knowledge about 'race' legislation or 'cultural differences' and disappeared in considerations of the generic basis of equalities

- Training content with a focus on personal attitudes to racism (race awareness training) appeared and then disappeared. It has reappeared in a different guise – one in which training is focused on individual differences and individual diversity

- Training has attempted to cover the whole question of organisational culture in a few hours.

In sum, training lacks clarity about race, racism, ethnicity and culture. It provides no understanding about the discourse of overt and covert racism. That racism is a force that shifts according to specific contexts and historical moments goes unrecognised. Training mirrors the social policy approach. The next chapter demonstrates how current social policy has failed to unravel racism. The increased demands for training following the Stephen Lawrence Inquiry will not necessarily impact on the racism in society unless social policy actively unravels all its forms.

A great deal of activity around racism has been generated by the Stephen Lawrence Inquiry. This may be a useful moment at which to examine the current policy context, since it will greatly influence the direction organisations take in designing educational or training interventions.

6

The Post-Stephen Lawrence Inquiry Policy Context

This chapter considers recommendations from the Stephen Lawrence Inquiry, particularly those on training to combat racism. Despite the government's good will and sincere concern about racism, responses so far are flawed by their failure to understand the pervasive and shifting nature of racism. Analysis of current social policy in relation to racism reveals contradictions which limit the effectiveness of training. Worse still, the social policy context may even entrench racism. The government adopts a managerial approach to policy development and implementation. This has the effect of depoliticising racism. Social policy initiatives are therefore misconceived and force strategists and policy makers to revert to old approaches to challenging racism, approaches which have proved to be erroneous.

This chapter considers the wider context in social policy for training to combat racism. How is the content of training to combat racism proscribed by government policy and discourse? How is the content pre-empted by institutions, such as large public sector bodies and voluntary sector organisations? How can we use our understanding of government and organisational policy to design appropriate educational interventions? How can we engage in critical thinking on racism so that limitations of social policy are acknowledged? The chapter considers responses to the Stephen Lawrence Inquiry and the policy of the Social Exclusion Unit, since these are the avenues through which race has recently been addressed in social policy.

Public policy since the Stephen Lawrence Inquiry

For many commentators and activists, the Inquiry on Stephen's murder provided a space within which to refocus public attention towards the enduring problem of racism. The Inquiry Report stated that the Metropolitan Police was institutionally racist.

A well organised campaign by the Lawrence family and its supporters created a media discourse which enabled '*debates that had long been confined to race professionals and academics... (to enter) ...widely into public consciousness*' (Cohen 1999 p. 10). These debates concerned the concept of institutional racism and its wide definition. The Report emphasised organisational procedures and the frequently unwitting, unintentional nature of institutional racism. The report was itself subject to a great deal of media attention. The findings and recommendations were seen as resonating from the past and carrying far-reaching implications for the future. The push by the Lawrence family for a private prosecution, the incompetence and inadequacy of the internal investigation of the murder inquiry (the Barker Review), the public inquest and the report of the Police Complaints Authority, contributed to the sequence of events leading to the Inquiry. The refusal by his family and friends to give up ensured that the murder of Stephen Lawrence, and other young men of African Caribbean and South Asian origin whose deaths or attacks evoked poor official police responses, remained stubbornly on the pages of our newspapers.

Recommendations and Action Plan

The campaign and subsequent Inquiry forced the Government to engage in a wide-ranging parliamentary debate. The Home Secretary responded with a detailed Action Plan of the seventy recommendations (Home Office 1999). The Action Plan sets out each recommendation in the Inquiry Report and lists actions to be taken with regard to each one.

The recommendations of the Report were far-reaching. They included reforming the Race Relations Act so that it is extended to the police and other public bodies. There is emphasis on creating greater accountability in recognising and monitoring racist incidents; in

Stop and Search incidents; in recruitment and retention of senior police officers; in creating better inspections of the police and in reviewing training and awareness raising.

The first set of recommendations in the Inquiry Report deal with openness and accountability and concern the need to restore the trust of the 'ethnic minority communities' in policing. The Report recommends setting performance indicators on the nature, extent and effectiveness of racism awareness training in the police (p.327). The Report condemns the failure of police training to combat racism (p.30) and makes six separate recommendations on training to combat racism and value cultural diversity (48–54). Recommendation 54 states:

> That consideration be given to a review of the provision of training in racism awareness and valuing cultural diversity in local government and other agencies including other sections of the Criminal Justice System. (p.333)

Although the majority of the Report's recommendations relate to the police, there are also clear recommendations for other public agencies. These include amending the national curriculum, and encouraging schools and local authorities to plan strategies to address racism, by reviewing policies and their outcomes in relation to black and other ethnic minority communities (p.321).

Recommendations about training and education

The Home Secretary set up a review of racism awareness training in response to Recommendation 54. It is anticipated that there will be a report in the next year or so (Institute of Employment Studies 2000). The brief for the review asks researchers to carry out a desk-based review of literature, identify existing practice in six sectors and carry out case studies in organisations in order to identify the factors associated with success, presumably raising awareness (Research Briefing IES 2000).

Recommendation 54 relates to other recommendations in the Report, such as Recommendation 24 urging the training of family liaison officers in racism awareness and cultural diversity. These recommendations on training have been made as a knee-jerk response to the rediscovery of police racism. Training to combat racism has been going on for over twenty years, but has been found to be ineffective. The very idea of training to combat racism has to be questioned. Government policy on race is neither reflective nor analytic – speedy responses have been made to the Inquiry due to public pressure; the recommendations and analysis have been accepted wholesale. In relation to training, there has been a failure to consider and re-evaluate social policy itself. Although the Institute of Employment Studies is carrying out a review of training to combat racism, it is argued that the review will not necessarily engage with the wider dimensions of social policy, or even analyse the nature and shifting forms of racism. It may already be limited by its focus on existing practice in training, rather than grappling conceptually with race and social policy and how we measure success.

The national context on race

The Stephen Lawrence Inquiry generated a flurry of positive responses to the findings and 70 key recommendations for change. In October 1999, Cabinet Office Minister Mo Mowlam announced a 'Better government for Ethnic Minorities' programme to increase the pace of progress on equality issues in the public sector. In the same week, it was announced that the Greater London Assembly will have a duty to promote equal opportunities, and the Mayor of London will have to report annually on progress on fighting racism and other forms of discrimination.

The Local Government Association, the Employers Organisation and the Improvement and Development Agency for local government have produced guidance on the implications for Local Government. This urges all local government that

> Race equality must be a key part of our political and managerial agenda for change ... The Guidance aims to encourage local authorities as employers to address and prevent racism, racial harassment and prejudice; promote and value ethnic and cultural diversity; and to ensure that Black, Asian and other ethnic minority people are treated fairly. It also aims to support local authorities in their role as community leaders, and as planners, providers and contractors of services, to ensure that Black, Asian and other ethnic minority people, including

refugees and asylum seekers, receive services that are appropriate, accessible and fairly distributed (Hunt and Palmer 1999).

As we shall see, the social policy context is positive on the one hand, in that we now have legislation and an action plan to promote race equality. On the other hand, we are witnessing a stream of legislation and political discourse which fuels racism and which excludes a whole range of minorities from feeling British. The contradictions in promoting race equality and undermining it at the same time needs to be understood when thinking about racism. We look in detail at the positive attempts to promote race equality and consider the legislation that contradicts these efforts.

Legislation

Current or proposed legislation which has race discrimination at its core has brought race back onto the public policy agenda. Within the public sector, the Race Relations Amendment Act, which will require public bodies to promote race equality as a statutory duty, comes into force in April 2001. The police service will have to comply with the Macpherson recommendation that the full force of race relations legislation should apply to all police officers. Furthermore, all chief police officers will be liable for acts or omissions by their officers (Recommendation 11). As a result of campaigning by many groups, including the Commission for Racial Equality, the government was forced into amending the Bill to include indirect discrimination (CRE 2000).

Also significant is the legislation that affects local government and the public sector, including the 1998 Human Rights Act, which came into force in October 2000. For the first time, individuals have the right to enforce their European Convention rights in UK courts. The right to be free of discrimination and the right to liberty and security, freedom of conscience, thought and religion and the right to a fair trial are among the rights included in the Convention. Spencer (2000) has written about the implications of the Human Rights Act in relation to race or racism. She argues that the right to family life may enable families to challenge their separation by immigration controls or deportation. Freedom from degrading treatment may provide an additional ground on which to challenge discriminatory treatment or harassment. In each case the Act protects people from religious and racial discrimination in the enjoyment of their rights. These rights are, however, not absolute:

> In certain circumstances ... public authorities will be able to argue that it was necessary to restrict rights in order to protect the rights of others. But that infringement will have to be proportional to the harm they are trying to prevent. Thus the police could exercise their powers to ban a fascist march, restricting freedom of assembly in order to prevent crime and disorder; but to ban any march, where no threat of disorder existed, would be disproportional and thus unlawful (Spencer 2000).

Together, the Race Relations Amendments Act and the Human Rights Act set a culture for promoting equality and strengthening group and individual rights.

Other social policy initiatives, however, work directly against reducing inequality and tackling discrimination. Policy changes on asylum, legislation restricting freedom of information and the right to trial by jury, as well as policies on social exclusion are analysed below. All are examples of government legislation and policy that run counter to the encouragement of positive attitudes to cultural diversity and the countering of racism.

Most significant is the Immigration and Asylum Act (1999). Carriers' liability and visa sanctions before entry will prevent many endangered people from fleeing even the countries internationally recognised for their abysmal human rights record. Those who do arrive will be subject to poverty, exclusion and separation from a supportive community. The support package will be the equivalent of 70% of income support rate – this is about £36 per week for an adult. Only 10% will be paid in cash, the rest in vouchers (Rutter 2001). The dispersal policy compels asylum seekers to be spread out over the country, where they may be isolated and more vulnerable to hostility. Provision for them is likely to be poor, since local government has not been given resources to handle extra housing and benefit needs. Already the Refugee Council notes that dispersal is not working and people are returning to where they have compatriots, chiefly in London (Rutter 2001). The debate in the popular press has fuelled racism and cries of 'spongers', 'bogus', 'unwelcome', 'foreigners', 'anxious to live off the State' scream from the tabloids. It can be argued that the Act has effectively fuelled racism.

Legislation currently going through parliament on freedom of information may well institutionalise indifference in matters related to racism. It has been argued that the Bill exempts the police from having to make full disclosure of their actions in all areas of policing despite the recommendations made by Macpherson (Sivanandan, February 2000):

> Worse still, it has shut the door once more on police accountability. If the Lawrences' long struggle highlighted anything, it was the way police withheld vital information, covered up for one another, closed ranks and took no responsibility for their mistakes (Sivanandan 2000: 4).

This restriction in access to information extends to areas such as getting information about black deaths in police custody. There has been little dismantling of stop and search, to which young black men are five or six times more likely than white men to be subjected. The bill to abolish the right of defendants to jury trial for offences such as minor theft, criminal damage and assault will have a greater impact on black people since they are over-represented in such cases and have historically received the most severe sentences. All these developments confirm and exacerbate institutional racism (Sivanandan 2000). The families of black men who have been subject to racist attacks, such as Michael Menson and Ricky Reel, have had to tread the same road as the Lawrences did, as the police deny the possible motive of racism.

Education and training

In the 1990s, education and training for a multi-ethnic society has been missing from the agenda. A deracialised approach to social policy evolved over the 1980s, and became entrenched by the Conservative government (Gillborn 1997; Mac an Ghaill 1999). Race and racism were absent from New Labour's initial policy commitments and manifesto. A search of the manifesto and other key policy documents on the Party's own interactive database discovered no reference to racism (Gillborn 1997).

Although it is now mentioned in reports on social exclusion and in, for example, the report on *Excellence in Schools*, race inequality is an add-on (Gillborn, Youdell and Kirton 1999). The National Curriculum has been criticised as being narrow and elitist, with little emphasis on multiculturalism or racism, but no changes have been made. The Government's response to Recommendation 67 of the Stephen Lawrence inquiry that the National Curriculum should be amended to take account of valuing cultural diversity and preventing racism has been 'complacent in the extreme' (Runnymede Trust 2000).

This complacency is pushing strong religious groups such as Muslims to protest at the neglect by schools of their religion and culture. The rising numbers of racist attacks against people of South Asian origin, coupled with the absence on the curriculum of languages other than European ones, legitimates the racialisation of Muslims (Mac and Ghaill 1999). The campaign for separate schools has been the culmination of these frustrations. The fact that there are state-sponsored Catholic, Church of England and Jewish schools, whereas Muslims were refused them, added to the anger. Finally the Secretary of State for Education and Employment accepted applications for grant maintained status for Muslim schools in Birmingham, Brent and London with public funding (Mac an Ghaill 1999; Carvel 1998). There is also a Sikh and a Hindu school and an erstwhile private school for Seventh Day Adventists has been allowed to opt into the state sector. This defensive response only serves to entrench notions of the 'other'. It ignores problems of the rights of children to an education which is secular, and which allows them to exercise choice about their identities, religious and cultural. The support by Government for separate schools is a weak response. Ignoring, as this does, the deeper problem of racism in education, religious separatism only serves to entrench and 'fix' culture and race, exacerbating racialised divisions.

Nation and Britishness

Black people are still excluded from the notion of the British nation. In the New Labour election campaign in 1997, symbols of Empire like the British bulldog were resurrected, stressing *'a strong sense of history and tradition'* (*The Guardian* 28.3. 2000). Although the Prime Minister has attempted to present the Union flag as an inclusive idea of Britishness (*The Guardian* 28.3.2000), specific mention of ethnicity, multiculturalism or gender is not made in his argument and he presents it as gender neutral. There have been isolated attempts to include a positive idea of blackness or multiculturalism in some government speeches (see Gordon Brown in Alibhai-Brown 1999: 1, or Mike O'Brien's speech in Alibahi-Brown 1999 p. 7). Some notable attempts have been made by young black people born here to reclaim Britishness and Indianness/Caribbeanness. However, the coded language of who is British and who is excluded remains, albeit in a more fragmented form, and is still subject to contestation:

> Britishness has systematic and largely unspoken racialised connotations. Whiteness of course nowhere appears as a condition of membership. But everyone understands that Englishness, and Britishness by extension, is racially coded. There ain't no black in the Union Jack (Gilroy 1987 quoted in Hall 2000 p. 21).

Such exclusion from being British or from full citizenship has important implications for the very idea of race, which legitimised racism. Colour is the foundation by which Britishness is constructed. This unspoken racialised connotation is brought more to the fore when outsiders are spoken about in dominant discourse, particularly asylum seekers. The media's panic about asylum seekers has fuelled common-sense racism. The new regulations place asylum seekers in a trap. They are told not to seek work *and* not to be dependent on the State – and this has become a topic for party political point scoring.

> Foreigners do not arrive by plane or train; they 'invade,'swamp' 'flood', 'pour in' or 'take over' – they are soldiers of an enemy onslaught (*The Guardian* 2 May 2000).

Calls for better immigration controls and protests about Britain being a 'soft touch' abound. People in Kent who felt they were bearing the brunt of 'financial strain' responded with even fiercer racism than the tabloids. Their racism was explicitly exposed by a complaint by Simon Hughes MP to the Commission for Racial Equality and the issue was debated in the press and media. Journalists and trade unionists such as Bill Morris accused government and political parties of fuelling racism. The debate centred on newcomers' dependence on British people's money and jobs and the matter of begging.

This panic and fear is not really about jobs, since the global labour market encourages labour mobility and indeed seeks to attract specialised skilled or unskilled labour, particularly from the developing world (*The Guardian*, 2.5.2000; *The Economist*, May 6 2000). For example, there is a shortage of 30,000 Information Technology specialists so they are being recruited from India; low level service work in cleaning, childcare, sweatshop or fast food delivery are jobs local people do not want to take, so European countries are turning a blind eye to 'illegal immigrants' whose menial labour is desperately needed. The panic and fear lies not in newcomers taking jobs away from those who have lived here longer; the panic and fear lies in the nature of the crisis of the nation state. The hidden discourse is about nationhood. Ideas of nation state and sovereignty are strengthened if we can keep people out or make them feel unwelcome. There is a fear that Britishness/Frenchness/Americanness is being undermined, since '*increased numbers of immigrants weaken the foundation of loyalty to the State, muddying it with loyalty to other states.*' (Nigel Harris *The Guardian* 2 May 2000).

This emphasis on being British, together with belonging and citizenship, are central to an understanding of racism. The discourse on nationhood helps to racialise those who are entering Britain for the first time. As we have noted, the discourse about the relationship of immigration to bettering race relations has been a theme in politics since immigrants began arriving in the twentieth century. An association with racism and colour pervades current arguments.

Social exclusion

Another key government policy has been to stress the desirability of an inclusive meritocratic society. To this end there has been a growing discourse about social exclusion, although what exclusion means in this context is arguably exclusion from work. The Social Exclusion Unit in the Cabinet Office was established in 1997. Reports have been published on the homeless, truancy, the unemployed, crime and school exclusions, among other matters.

The government has stated that there is a growing indication of 'a more divided country' in the last two years, with higher living standards for many areas contrasted with the poorest neighbourhoods which continue to run down, becoming more prone to crime and more cut off from the labour market (see *Bringing Britain Together*, HMSO 1998 p.1). Although social and economic changes have played their part, there have also been failures in urban policy initiatives and past government policies (HMSO 1998). Key factors which exacerbate the divide include failure to deal with the structural causes of decline, parachuting solutions in from outside rather than engaging with local communities, and placing too much emphasis on physical renewal instead of creating opportunities for local people.

The approach to social problems and social inequalities is clearly exacerbating the problems. Firstly, complex social problems are posed in terms of society and the excluded alone:

> They address a nation of stakeholders who are positioned by social differences – or where the only difference is between society and the excluded. The complexity and instability of divisions and inequalities ... disappear (Clarke and Newman 1997: 156).

In fact, the subsuming of all inequalities under the exclusion label is intensely problematic. The examination of the different ways in which inequalities are produced and reproduced neutralises and de-politicises social policy. It de-genders and de-racialises political issues. So for example, 'wives and mothers' (from Beveridge) become 'parents and carers' (Clarke and Newman 1997). Problems that originate externally, such as the issue of racism, become problems that are defined as internal or as located in specific areas such as the inner city, where ethnic minorities tend to be concentrated (Lewis 2000). The issue of class has all but disappeared from our language and actions, yet it exerts a powerful influence in relation to the decline of manual work, homelessness, health and other issues. Class is not openly discussed, but the emphasis on young working class people to conform to an inclusive society based on a heteronormative family and regular work patterns form the thrust of all policy initiatives.

These strategies and plans are only challenged when there is a public outcry, such as the Stephen Lawrence inquiry, or when gender gaps in pay hit the headlines, forcing some accommodation to the plans and a cry for an explicit recognition of the effects of race and gender.

Managerialism

De-politicisation of this kind is integral to the creation of a managerial state (Clarke and Newman 1997). Consequently, the Social Exclusion Unit adopts a managerial approach to policy itself. The de-politicised approach affects not only the ways in which institutions should be structured but also the thinking about in-equalities and the contradictions inequalities may pose for policy formation. The fragmentation of social communities across several axes of class, gender, race and/or disability are not taken into account, so they come to be problems of homelessness, truancy, ex-clusion and crime – problems that have to be managed.

> Managerial discourse offers particular representations of the relation-ship between social problems and solutions. It is linear and oriented to single goal thought patterns. It is concerned with goals and plans rather than with intentions and judgements. It is about action rather than reflection. It draws on analysis (breaking problems down) rather than synthesis (Clarke and Newman 1997 p.148).

As these authors point out, the use of the terms efficiency (whose efficiency?), effectiveness (effectiveness for whom?), performance and quality displace political choices into managerial imperatives (Clarke and Newman 1997). This condensation of all social divi-sions into one category inevitably leads to charges of colour blind-ness, as highlighted in the Stephen Lawrence Inquiry.

Reports on social exclusion published before the Inquiry hardly mentioned race or any other social divisions. Pressure and cam-paigns to make racism more explicit in government policy on social exclusion has put ethnic minority communities under the microscope. The pragmatic approach to race suggests a government committed not to challenging inequalities but rather to managing them through discourse or league tables. Consequently, when race is included in government policies it is not understood.

The *relations* of inequality between the excluded and included, across social divisions, are not examined. The focus is placed on the excluded, who are then constructed as problems. For example, in the chapter headings of one report, we find a half page entitled 'Is there an ethnic minority effect?', which consists of a series of statistical statements about the effects of poverty on black communities (Social Exclusion Unit Policy Action Team No 12: Young People March 2000 p.27). This pattern runs through the documents. When racism is mentioned it is as an add-on, separated from 'the norm'.

There is widespread amnesia about Britain's history and how race was implicated in it (Fryer 1984) – in colonialism, in the immigration acts against Irish, Jewish and black populations, in the setting up of the Welfare State through post-war immigration. Yet race has clearly been part of the way British society has continually reproduced inequalities (Lewis 2000). Race and racism cannot be written about as an add-on. It goes far deeper than that and is integral to Britain's history.

The repercussions are everywhere. Take, for example, school exclusions. A wealth of information has been developed over the last twenty years about teacher attitudes and expectations towards black children, whom they view in racially stereotyped ways (Lewis 2000). This dynamic is played out between teachers and children, in the classroom and playground. One would therefore imagine that action for change would focus on training teachers in relation to their interactions with children, black and white, in schools and the reproduction of stereotypes, whether about children of African Caribbean origin, South Asian origin and so on. Yet the recommendations in the report on school exclusions from the SEU focuses on only one side of this interaction and merely describes working with families and parents in the black communities and in mentoring schemes, or discusses the underachievement of black children, particularly those of African Caribbean origin (Lewis 2000).

Race is once again viewed here in social policy terms as something we have to do to black communities or black families, thus entrenching them as the problem. Where the issue is reducing exclusions, the recommendations adopt managerial discourse: data collection and behaviour management in learning curricula for teacher training, rather than challenging racial stereotyping.

Public knowledge about the performance of organisations, it is argued, will compel organisations to change, become more efficient and more accountable, particularly in the public sector; thus data collection is needed to track and monitor change. But these initiatives are again part of a technicist discourse that does not allow for reflection or the consideration of political choices. The discourse stresses measuring outcomes and fails to aid thinking about the means. Thus the number of exclusions may decrease, but this may have no effect on racial stereotyping or on creating teachers who are more aware. We may want an outcome where teachers and others have a variety of perceptions of black children and white which transcend ideas of race. In fact, we may see figures which show decreases in exclusions, but this may be because children of African Caribbean origin are more likely to be unofficially excluded so do not appear in the statistics because they are being kept in special centres within schools (Bhavnani and Foot 2000).

The relationship between problem analysis and the means by which the problem is solved has been severed. The policies are misconceived because they are based on the assumption that all social issues can be cut up into their various constituent parts, action plans defined and targets set.

Conclusions

This discussion has highlighted several key issues:

- A raft of measures exist which reinforce racism and counter legislation on Human Rights and the Race Relations Amendment Bill to promote race equality and reduce discrimination. These include the jeopardised right to jury trial and freedom of information. Race is missing from many other aspects of government policy and from speeches made by Ministers. The policy and legislation on asylum seekers fuels racism.

- Policies designed to challenge race equality in social exclusion policy are misconceived on several counts. They do not consider the differential impacts of race, gender, class, disability and sexuality and they subsume all those who are excluded under a single label. Such approaches are part of a managerial approach to social policy that stresses goals and plans rather than intentions, judgements or understandings of different issues and how they relate to each other. They fail to take account of how these social divisions have been part of the way British society has developed over the centuries and why they therefore have to be integrally and specifically addressed in social policy. On the rare occasions they are considered, they are an add-on.

- The wider context of such social policy profoundly affects training about racism. Where discussion of race inequality is absent, the discourse resorts to the tolerance by and meritocracy of society. This characterises the colour-blind approach. It was certainly apparent in much of the police discourse on racism in the Stephen Lawrence Inquiry. On the other hand, now that race is being openly discussed, strategies focus on black families and communities as the problem. The focus is not where it needs to be: on the social relations between majority groups who have power and minority groups who may have less, nor on the intersection of social divisions based on class, race or gender.

- This lack of clarity in social policy has been influenced by misconceptions. Ideas of race, ethnicity, culture, nation and the changing nature of racism have not been understood. Training reflects social policy. If we are to have effective training we need some conceptual clarity within government policy. Government has to unravel racism before society can move forward.

7

Conclusions and Recommendations

Since the early 1980s, millions of pounds have been spent on training to combat racism. Yet it is clear from the present analysis that the training has failed. It has failed because, all too often, its content and approach has been developed in isolation from an understanding of racism in British society as a whole.

Unravelling racism

Understanding and unravelling the constantly changing nature of racism is crucial to developing an effective approach to education and training on combating it. The Stephen Lawrence Inquiry attempted to shift the debate from distorted conceptions of racism in social policy by identifying the nature of racism in the Metropolitan police as institutional racism. This has placed the focus on (white-dominated) organisations – their processes, procedures and outcomes.

There are dangers in such an approach. For racism concerns ideologies as well as structures and processes. It is about power, about racial and ethnic inequality. Racism is reproduced and re-created in a variety of contexts – at work, on the streets, in the home, in the playground and classroom and elsewhere. It is reproduced through our everyday relations. If institutional racism becomes a justification for taking responsibility away from the individuals with power and if it is perceived to be 'unwitting' will always be denied. Senior policy makers can absolve themselves of responsibility for its reproduction. Yet individuals make and re-make their own identities in relation to wider political and social processes. They are agents in reproducing or challenging racism.

If the concept of institutional racism is used in such a way that organisational procedures are reviewed as if no human agency were involved and as if the organisation and the individuals within it operate in isolation from wider society, then it will not be helpful. Training based on such an approach fails to assist people in understanding the expressions and contexts of racism within their specific localities – schools, streets, offices, hospitals, banks and families. It will fail to assist in the nature of gendered and classed racisms. It may fail to take account of the fact that racism operates in a historically and politically specific fashion. For example, the racism experienced by African Americans in the USA during the early part of the 20th century is different from the racism experienced by immigrants from the ex-colonies in Britain after World War II. Racism is not just about the dislike of foreigners. We cannot eliminate racism on the assumption that once we understand differences in culture – i.e. cultures different from *our own* – it will automatically be challenged and ultimately vanish.

Racism cannot be reduced to mere concern about personal liking and understanding. This simplistic aproach fails to explore how racisms are linked and intertwined with dominant discourse and how racism shifts according to its context and its visibility/invisibility in discourse. The racism of the British National Party is highly visible but it is not the most prevalent form of racism in Britain. Yet it is constructed as if it were the defining racism. Other racisms are present, some more visible than others at particular times, and these are reflected in social policy. For example, there is the racism related to immigration policies and asylum-seekers and the racism by which Britishness operates primarily as a code for whiteness.

Some manifestations of racism may be completely hidden from view. They exist in the form of absences. For example, there is the racism involved in ignoring its very existence; of sidelining it or of maintaining that it originates and operates only in inner cities, or only where there are black people.

Unpacking social policy

Examining social policy and understanding the wider social policy context helps to illuminate the current limitations of training to combat racism and will ultimately improve educational interventions. The misconceptions in social policy originate from the failure to understand the nature of racism or to unravel it effectively. By and large, social policy in relation to race has concentrated on black minority groups and their families. It has viewed blackness as the problem, interpreted blackness as ethnicity and translated blackness into 'culture'.

These misconceptions in social policy have had two key effects. Firstly, race is perceived as an add-on to other issues in British social relations. Race and racism are marginalised in social policy and consequently marginalised in training. Secondly, masking the idea of 'whiteness' and its cultures and ethnicities has masked power – its locus and operation.

Discovering racism through discourse

By exploring the specificities of racism through discourse, the full spectrum of racisms can be revealed. If we only see racism operating in one particular way or one specific area we shall fail to challenge it as a whole and any interventions will have little success. The Lawrence Inquiry transcripts demonstrate that alongside the racism in the white working class estates of the inner city, there existed a managerial and professional racism among officers at every level of the Metropolitan Police Force, a racism that legitimated whiteness as the norm and was characterised by a strong culture of denial at the highest levels. And even among the lawyers, understanding of racism was incomplete.

The limitations of current training

Training to combat racism has moved in tandem with social policy initiatives, legislation and a wider consensus about the nature of racism. How racism is viewed has shifted from a scientific notion of race to one that is culturally defined. The new racism is 'cultural' racism and is more covert, more difficult to demonstrate tangibly. Covert racism remains hidden and is contested in a variety of ways.

It has been recently described as the unwitting, unintentional operation of procedures and processes. Yet it is also about conscious or unconscious stereotyping; it can construct different ethnic groups differently in relation to male/female and working class/middle class. There are a variety of overt and covert gendered and classed racisms. These differing contexts of racism and their historical specificity are impossible to tackle effectively in a short training course to combat racism.

Secondly, training has, in the main, *reinforced* social policy rather than challenged it. Whatever the desired outcomes of training – assimilation, integration, positive action – training to combat racism has problematised the position of black minorities and their families. It has focused on black minorities and their cultures. It has taken a 'tolerance' approach – of understanding the experience of the 'other' and learning tolerance for 'other cultures'. But the very word tolerance suggests something defined as outside of the norm, that has to be endured, tolerated. It is assumed that educating white people about facts about other people's cultures and about relevant legislation will ensure that they will then act meritocratically in a meritocratic society. This approach has rendered training meaningless, since those being trained often see no reason why challenging racism has anything to do with them when, after all, it is black minorities whom they see as the key recipients of action on racism.

Improving educational interventions

Education to combat racism should not be a way of mirroring social policy. As indicated above, social policy needs to be unpacked so that misconceptions can be exposed. Education must be involved in a critique of social policy. The limited ways in which social policy addresses racism, including the emphasis primarily on black people, fails to engage with the *relations* of inequality. These relations can be made visible at all levels in society and in all contexts by unravelling different racisms.

Covert racism can be exposed and unmasked through discourse. Dominant discourse in the media, by senior managers and policy makers and in Parliament frequently legitimates the expression of overt racism. Education must develop a critical approach to dominant discourse in social policy and the media. It must expose different racisms reproduced through discourse, which may be differentiated by gender, age, class, nationalism and occupational culture.

A long-term analysis of different racisms may help us to achieve better educative results. Training is too short term and does not have implicit in it a long-term educative objective. A long-term analysis of racisms and ongoing open discussions will help us to get closer to effectively targeting strategies for combating them in their different forms. Analysing these specific contexts of racism, in and outside work organisations can, for example, enable us to pinpoint different groups who hold differing access to power in British society and who may need differing interventions. A long-term analysis of occupational cultures can enable us to make strategic decisions about where to intervene, when, how and with whom. It is beyond the scope of this book to suggest a detailed framework of how this analysis might be done. However, what is clear is that training initiatives as currently carried out are not embedded in a long-term strategic examination of how racism is produced and reproduced in organisational cultures and processes. They do not include *everyone* in the process of changing fundamental structures and social constructions to combat racism. It is very difficult to challenge racism through training that is not part of a long-term strategy.

Effective education must deal with both the specific and the wider context of racism, and with the connections between them. Off-the-shelf training seems pretty well irrelevant, since it makes no effort to analyse the context of racisms for the organisations and individuals involved. Any programme of effective education must examine relationships of power between and within the groups, within the organisation as well as in the wider society, and the ways these are expressed and experienced.

People and organisations have to try to understand how racism takes many different shapes and forms and how these forms are linked. Understanding and analysing these contexts may help to make sense of racism and its relevance to those participating in the education. It is unlikely that such understanding can be gained wholly in a short module in the classroom, or by attending short training courses.

How do we measure better educative results concerning racism? Satisfactory results should really be measured in terms of long-term vision. We should be aiming for a situation where we can understand the need to go beyond race in our everyday interactions. We must aim to keep our identities open and resist attempts to close them, such that blackness or whiteness does not remain a key determinant of our interactions. We must resist a fixity of ascribed singular ethnic identities such as Indian, English, Irish, Caribbean, Chinese, Somali etc, and discuss the multiple identities we bring to interactions, by gender, class, age and sexuality. We must challenge ourselves and others when we or others behave according to allocated stereotypical roles. In doing so, we must be involved in exposing power and the ways in which we may be controlled and categorised by those who hold power. We must therefore be open, inclusive and democratic.

A longer-term educative approach is required to *unlearning* racism while learning about it. The business of raising awareness should be about enabling people to understand why racism matters, why it is relevant to everyone and why everyone has a role in challenging it. It must be about discovering ownership of its reproduction and ownership of the task of challenging it. Racism concerns us all.

Recommendations

Creating a culture of challenging racism

There is an urgent need to create a culture that legitimates discussing and debating racism in all its forms. A culture that is not colour blind and which does not pigeonhole racism as solely a problem of the 'inner cities'. Government must facilitate the development of such a culture by celebrating difference and challenging racism in education and teaching. This legitimation can be fostered in schools, and through policies that address inequality. Government needs to avoid announcements and policies that link restricting immigration with the idea of good race relations, for example, or that link refugees with 'spongers'.

1. Tackling racism in social policy

The government must ensure that the connections traditionally made between curbing immigration and good race relations are broken once and for all. It must face up to its own responsibility for reproducing racism or taking a lead in eradicating it.

2. Education for citizenship

The Crick Report on citizenship education has been criticised for its 'somewhat colonial flavour' (Osler 1999). The report states that due regard should be given to the homelands of our minority communities and to the main countries of British emigration in its discussion of national identity in a pluralist context. This, as Osler points out, precludes the idea that people have a variety of hybrid or multiple identities, which vary across contexts. Nor does the report make any mention of racism.

Schools have a crucial role in enabling national identities to be more inclusively constructed. Education for citizenship must involve identity construction, difference and *commonality*. It must not ignore racism, sexism and classism in the curriculum. It should make the link between participation in a democracy and challenging inequality. It must incorporate white ethnicities. Once these are incorporated into the teaching about citizenship it will be possible to celebrate cultural diversity.

3. The national curriculum

The association of the British imperial nation with ideas of white supremacy should be discussed within the national curriculum. This collective 'working through' (Hall 2000) a focus on whiteness and an idea of shared space is essential for people to take on multiculturalism without concomitant ideas of superiority. The national curriculum should be interrogated for its absence of teaching critically about slavery and colonialism and their effect on how masculinities and femininities have developed across class.

4. Social exclusion

The Social Exclusion Unit must be explicit about the interaction of poverty, class, race, age and gender, and construct its policies specifically in light of this interaction. The current approach of collapsing inequality and poverty into one framework means the same solutions are offered for differing ideologies and their impacts. Issues of power remain hidden. A link must also be made between processes and outcomes. These processes must include an understanding of power. For example, all teachers need to undergo training in classroom interaction and the reproduction of stereotypes so they can learn how to challenge racism. This curriculum content needs to form part of all teacher training and it should inform all in-service courses. All sides of these interactions (e.g. teacher, student, head teacher, parents) must be opened up for scrutiny.

5. Developing competences in professional and managerial training

Competences for all professional and managerial groups on challenging racism must be incorporated into their professional training. These should form a basis for career development and performance assessment.

6. Dealing with denial

The denial of racism within organisations must be addressed, before designing strategies or programmes for correcting it.

Training courses

Racism has been shown to be highly complex in its forms and expressions. It shifts and changes according to context. There are different racisms and they have to be analysed against specific contexts with a wider reference to history and the present. This cannot possibly be achieved in a training course lasting one or two days.

It is time for 'special' training courses and 'antiracist days' to end. It is clear that teaching about cultures in isolation from considering whiteness, superiority and ethnicity can well do more harm than good. The notion that racism is only about white versus black is misconceived. It assumes that this identity is always the most important one in understanding racism. It also reinforces a fixed nature of how racism operates and renders white ethnicities and divisions invisible. Teaching diversity as if it were merely about individual differences and there were no collective experience of shared discrimination does nothing to challenge racism.

An entirely different approach to awareness raising is required. The following recommendations suggest more creative approaches to raising awareness.

a. *Unravelling racisms within organisations*

Organisations and workplaces need to unravel the racism in their own contexts. They have to understand that organisations reproduce racism, and part of this understanding concerns how it is reproduced through dominant discourse and everyday racism.

b. *Discovering and challenging racism*

The skills required to intervene in the discovery and challenge of racism within specific contexts, in and out of organisations, are not necessarily the traditional training skills. There is a need for external advice and verification, so that racism and its reproduction can be examined and action can be taken. This may demand the skills of those who are independent of the organisation and help those within it to view organisational culture from a fresh perspective. Skills in organisation development and change management may need to sit alongside sound understanding about racisms and their manifestations. An effective programme might involve independent social audits that stress qualitative outcomes. There is a need for long-term work in this area to encourage critical thinking on racism.

c. *An inclusive and mainstream approach*

Any intervention to combat racism has to be inclusive. The strategy to combat racism has to question, be critical and say the unsayable. The relevance of racism to people's lives and work has to be made clear to all. Racism must not be sidelined from other initiatives to make changes in the organisational culture. It is imperative that all groups are involved in these processes, not just black minorities or white middle managers.

d. *Challenging racism within organisational cultures*

Intervention has to be relevant and must adopt a holistic approach. The few youth work projects which have effectively intervened and challenged racism indicate certain general tactics. In the case of the Bede project, for example, a general strategic approach to tackling racism was effectively agreed with the team, including the external adviser, but challenges to racism took place in the light of the agreed strategy, generated by the experience and needs of those on the receiving end and often not under the label 'training about racism'. It may mean that racism is not always explicitly discussed all the time; one may need to wait for the issue to be raised by those for whom the intervention is designed. In the Bede project, the young people were unwilling to raise the topic, so opportunities were created for racism to be discussed, without this being imposed from the outside.

Organisational cultures are maintained by certain expected un-written behaviours, stories and narratives which reveal how the informal aspects of the culture work. It may be worth exploring how to analyse the narratives and behaviours in organisations for what they reveal about racism. This idea needs further exploration and research to develop a more practical approach to intervention in organisational cultures.

Also worth considering is the possibility of managers working prac-tically with differing community groups, not just black voluntary sector groups but with the range of local community groups who address gender, race, sexuality and/or class issues in the course of their work. Placement with local community groups may provide important learning experiences for managers. In situations of this kind, racism is not something separate but is clearly ingrained in the context of doing and learning about difference and power among our diverse communities.

Bibliography

Aik Saath (1999) *Conflict Resolution in Slough for Young Asian People* Slough Borough Council

Alibahi-Brown Y (1999) *True Colours: Public Attitudes to Multiculturalism and the Role of Government* London: IPPR

Allen S (1973) The Institutionalisation of Racism *Race,* 15, July pp.99-105

Anthias F and Yuval-Davis N (1992) *Racialised Boundaries* London: Routledge

Back L (1994) *New Ethnicities and Urban Culture* London: UCL

Back L (1999) *Finding the Way Home – Working Papers no 5: rights and wrongs – youth community and narratives of racial violence* Centre for New Ethnicities Research (CNER), University of East London

Back L, Cohen P and Keith M (1999) *Finding the Way Home-Working Papers no 2: between home and belonging – critical ethnographies of race, place and identity* Centre for New Ethnicities Research (CNER), University Of East London

Baldwin P and Foot J (1998) *No Quality without Equality: Best Value and Equalities, The Local Government Best Value Partnership* LGMB: London and Luton

Barnsley Multi-Agency Panel *Racial Harassment Project Annual Report* June 1997 – June 1998

Bhavnani R (1994) *Black Women in the Labour Market: A Research Review* Manchester: Equal Opportunities Commission

Bhavnani R (1998) The Real Story on Black Women's Pay in *Visible Women Newsletter* No 2 November/December p.6 London: Commission for Racial Equality

Bhavnani R and Foot J (2000) *Race Matters in Lambeth: a Review of Race Equality* London Borough of Lambeth: London

Body-Gendrot S (1998) Now you see, now you don't: comments on Paul Gilroy's article, in *Ethnic and Racial Studies* vol. 21 no. 5 September 1998

Brah (1992) Difference, Diversity and Differentiation in J Donald and A Rattansi (eds.) *'Race', Culture and Difference* Buckingham: Open University Press

Bristol City Council (1999) *Bristol City Council's Response to the Macpherson Report* 13 April, Bristol City Council

Brunswick Group (2000) *Implementing Human Rights Senior Management Workshop* 8th February for Group 4 Corporate Citizenship London: Brunswick

Bulmer M and Solomos J (1998) Re-thinking ethnic and racial studies, in *Ethnic and Racial Studies* vol. 21 no. 5 September 1998

Carmichael S and Hamilton C (1967) *Black Power* Harmondsworth Penguin

Carvel J (1998) Muslim Schools get the Grants *The Guardian* 10 January.

Castells M (1996) *The Information Age: economy, society and culture Vol 1 The Rise of the Network Society*; Vol 2 *The Power of Identity*; Vol 3 *End of Millenium* Oxford: Blackwell

Castles S (1996) Australia: multi-ethnic community without nationalism? in Hutchinson J and Smith AD (eds) *Ethnicity* Oxford: Oxford University Press

Castles S and Vasta E (1996) Multi-cultural or Multi-racist Australia in Vasta E and Castles S (eds) *The Teeth are Smiling: the persistence of racism in multi-cultural Australia* St Leonards: Allen and Unwin

Castles S (1996) The Racisms of Globalisation in Vasta E and Castles S (eds) *op.cit.*

Clarke J and Newman J (1997) *The Managerial State* London: Sage

Cockburn C (1998) *The Space Between Us: negotiating gender and national identities in conflict* London: Zed Books

Cohen P (1997) Labouring Under Whiteness, in Frankenberg R *Displacing Whiteness* Durham: Duke University Press

Cohen P (1997) *Rethinking the Youth Question: education, labour and cultural studies* Basingstoke: Macmillan

Cohen P (1997) Getting through: new approaches to tackling youth racism, in CARF (Campaign against Racism and Fascism) *Bulletin* 1 November

Cohen P (1999) *Finding the Way Home – Working Papers no. 3: Strange encounters – adolescent geographies of risk and the urban uncanny* London: CNER

Cohen P (1999) Through a glass darkly: intellectuals on race, in Cohen P (ed) *New Ethnicities, Old Racisms* London: Zed Books

Commission for Racial Equality (1984) *A Report on the seminar on Racism Awareness Training held on 31 October 1984* London:CRE

Commission for Racial Equality (1991) *Open Talk, Open Minds: anti-racist education for young people* London:CRE

Commission for Racial Equality (1998) *Evidence to the Lawrence Inquiry Part 2* London:CRE

Commission for Racial Equality (1999) *CRE Factsheet: Racial attacks and harassment* London: CRE

Commission for Racial Equality (2000) *The Race Relations (Amendment) Bill: a briefing note following consideration in the House of Lords, February 2000* London:CRE

Connections (1999) *Young, white and wicked*, National Youth Agency, Leicester.

Cook V, Davis S and Wilson A (1999) *Domestic Violence Service Provision: Black Women's Perspectives* Race and Gender Research Unit: Luton University

Council of Europe (1996) *Tackling Racist and Xenophobic Violence in Europe: review and practical guidance* Berlin: Council of Europe

Coyle A (1995) Learning from Experience: The Equal Opportunities Challenge for the 1990s *The Seven Million Project Working Paper 5* London: DEMOS

The Crick Report (1998) *Education for Citizenship and the Teaching of Democracy in Schools* London: Qualifications and Curriculum Authority

Dadzie S (1997) *Blood, Sweat and Tears: an account of the Bede anti-racist detached youth work project* Leicester: Youth Work Press

Dadzie, S for Camden Race Equality Council (2000) *Visual Realities : A Guide for Teachers and Youth Workers* London: Camden Racial Equality Council

Dadzie S (2000) *Toolkit for Tackling Racism in Schools* Stoke-On-Trent: Trentham Books

Davies C (2000) The Demise of Professional Self Regulation: A moment to mourn? in Lewis G, Gewirtz S and Clarke J (eds) *Rethinking Social Policy* Open University and Sage: London Thousand Oaks New Delhi

Degaldo R and Stefancic J (eds) (1997) *Critical White Studies: looking beyond the mirror* Philadelphia: Temple University Press

Department of Environment Transport and the Regions (1999) *Local Government Act 1999: Part 1 Best Value 14 December* London: DETR

Department of Environment Transport and the Regions (1999) *New Deal for Communities Race Equality Guidance: Race Equality Guidance* October London: DETR

Dhalech M (1998) *Challenging Racism in the Rural Idyll: final report of the rural race equality project Cornwall, Devon and Somerset* Devon Youth Service

du Gay *et al* (1997) *Doing Cultural Studies: the story of the Sony Walkman* London: Sage

Dummett (1973) *A Portrait of English Racism* Harmondsworth: Penguin

Ellis C and Sonnenfield J (1994) Diverse Approaches to Managing Diversity *Human Resource Management* Spring 1994 vol. 33 no 1 pp79-109

Esland G (1980) Professions and Professionalism in Esland G and Salaman G (eds.) *The Politics of Work and Occupations* Milton Keynes: Open University Press

Essed P (1991) *Understanding Everyday Racism* London: Sage

Fanon F (1986) *Black Skins, White Masks* London: Penguin

Fenton S (1982) Multi Something Education *New Community* 10, 1, 57-63

Fine M (1997) Witnessing Whiteness in Fine M *et al* (eds) *Off White: readings on race, power and society* London: Routledge

Frankenberg R (1993) *White Women, Race Matters* London Routledge

Frankenberg R (1997) Introduction: Local Whiteness, Localising Whiteness, in Frankenberg R *Displacing Whiteness* Durham: Duke University Press

Fryer (1984) *Staying Power:The History of Black People in Britain* London: Pluto Press

Gillborn D (1997) Natural Selection: New Labour race and education policy in *MCT Multicultural Teaching* Vol 15, No 3

Gillborn D Youdell D and Kirton A(1999) Government Policy and School Effects: racism and social justice in policy and practice in *MCT Multicultural Teaching* Vol. 17, No 3

Gilroy P (1982) Police and Thieves, in Centre for Contemporary Cultural Studies (ed) *The Empire Strikes Back: Race and racism in 70s Britain* Hutchinson and CCCS: Birmingham

Gilroy P (1987) *There ain't no black in the Union Jack: the cultural politics of 'race' and nation* London: Hutchinson

Gilroy P (1992) The end of antiracism, in Donald J and Rattansi A (eds.) *'Race' Culture and Difference* London: Sage/Open University Press

Givens N, Almeida D, Holden C and Taylor B (1999) Swimming with the Tide: ethnic minority experiences in initial teacher education *MCT Multicultural Teaching* Vol 17, No 2

GLEA (2000) *The Organisational and managerial implications of developed personnel assessment processes: summary report* London: GLEA

Gurnah A (1984) The Politics of Racism Awareness Training *Critical Social Policy* Issue 11, pp.6-20

Hall S, Critcher C, Jefferson T, Clarke J and Roberts B (1978) *Policing the Crisis: Mugging, the State and Law and Order* London: Hutchinson

Hall S (1992a) New Ethnicities, in Donald J and Rattansi A (eds) *'Race', Culture and Difference* London: Sage/Open Univerity Press

Hall S (1992b) The Question of Cultural Identity, in Hall S, Held D and McGrew T (eds.) *Modernity and its Futures* London: Polity/Open University Press

Hall S (ed.) (1997) *Representation: cultural representations and signifying practices* London: Sage

Hall S (2000) Rethinking the National Story; paper prepared for the *Commission on the Future of Multiethnic Britain* London: Runnymede Trust

Haringey Council (1999) *Review of Race Equality Strategy – Future Action* 22 March

Her Majesty's Inspectorate of Constabulary (1999) *Winning the Race: Policing Plural Communities Revisited* London: Home Office

Hewitt R (1992) *Sagaland: a study of Youth Culture, Racism and Education – a report on research carried out in Thamesmead* London: Institute of Education, Centre for Multicultural Education

Hewitt R (1996) *Routes of Racism: the social basis of racist action* Stoke on Trent: Trentham Books

Hewstone M and Brown R (1986) Contact is not enough: an intergroup perspective on the 'contact' hypothesis in Hewstone M and Brown R (eds) *Contact and Conflict in Intergroup Encounters* Oxford: Blackwell

Hickman M (June 1999) *Writing 'race', invisibilising the Irish in Britain – reversing this process as a strategy for a achieving a multi-ethnic Britain (Parts 1 and 2)* London: Runnymede Trust

Holdaway S (2000) Police Race Relations – *paper for the Commission on Multi Ethnic Britain* London: Runnymede Trust

Hollands RG (1990) *The Long Transition: class, culture and youth training* Basingstoke: Macmillan

Home Office (1999) *Police Training: a Consultation Document* Home Office November

Home Office (1999) *Statistics on Race and the Criminal Justice System* Home Office Research, Development and Statistics Directorate

Home Office (2000a) *Race Equality in Public Services* Home Office

Home Office (2000b) *Stephen Lawrence Inquiry: Home Secretary's Action Plan. First Annual Report on Progress* Home Office Communication Directorate

Honeyford R (1988) *Integration or Disintegration? Towards a non-racist society* London: Claridge Press

hooks b (1989) *Talking Back* London: Sheba

Hughes S (10 April 2000) Letter of Complaint to the Commission for Racial Equality

Humphrey D and John G (1971) *Because they're Black* Harmondsworth: Penguin

Hunt J and Palmer S (June 1999) *The Stephen Lawrence Inquiry and Home Secretary's Action Plan: initial guidance for Local Authorities* LGA

Hunt J and Palmer S (November 1999) *The Stephen Lawrence Inquiry: further guidance for Local Authorities* LGA

Hunt J and Palmer S (February 2000) *The Stephen Lawrence Inquiry: further guidance for local authorities* LGA

Institute for Employment Studies (2000) *Training in Racism Awareness and Valuing Cultural diversity* Research Briefing IES March

John G (1970) *Race and the Inner City* London: Runnymede Trust

John G (2000) *Tackling Institutional Racism – a year post the Macpherson Inquiry Report: the Scottish Education Response* Centre for Education for Racial Equality in Scotland 25th February

Johnson MRD (February 1999) *Ethnicity and Health: Towards the future of a Healthy Multi-Ethnic Britain – a paper for the Commission on the Future of Multi-Ethnic Britain* London: Runnymede Trust

Kandola R and Kandola P (1995) Managing Diversity: new broom or old hat? in *International Review of Industrial and Organisational Psychology* vol. 10

Karve C and Vasista V (June 1999) *Submission to the Commission on the Future of Multi-Ethnic Britain on UK Compliance with international standards on Race Equality* London: Commission on the Future of Multi-Ethnic Britain

Katz J (1985) *White Awareness: handbook for anti-racism training* University of Oklahoma Press

Keith M (1999) *Finding the Way Home – Working papers no. 4: Making safe – young people community safety and racial danger* London: CNER

Kelly E (1988) Pupils, Racial Groups and Behaviour in Schools in Kelly E and Cohn C *Racism in Schools – New Research Evidence* Stoke on Trent: Trentham Books

Kirklees Metropolitan Council (1999) Kirklees Housing Services Draft Equality Policy: *Consultation Document* Kirklees Metropolitan Council

Leeds City Council 1999) *Developing a Racial Equality in Contracts Scheme* Leeds City Council February

Lewis G (2000) Discursive Histories, the Pursuit of Multiculturalism and Social Policy in Lewis G Gewirtz S and Clarke J (eds.) *Rethinking Social Policy* London: Sage/Open University

Lipsitz G (1998) T*he Possessive Investment in Whiteness: how white people profit from identity politics* Philadelphia: Temple University Press

Local Government Management Board (1997) *Equalities Performance Indicators: Draft* London: Local Government Management Board

Luthra M and Oakley R (1991) *Combating Racism through Training: a review of approaches to race training in organisations* ESRC no 22

Mac an Ghail M (1999) *Contemporary Racisms and Ethnicities* Buckingham and Philadelphia: Open University Press

Macdonald I *et al* (1989) *Murder in the Playground: The Report of the Macdonald Inquiry into Racial Violence in Manchester Schools* London: Longsight Press

Macey M (1995) Towards Racial Justice? A re-evaluation of anti racism in *Critical Social Policy* 44/45 Autumn pp.126-146

Macpherson W *et al* (1999) *The Stephen Lawrence Inquiry: report of an inquiry by Sir William Macpherson of Cluny* London: Stationery Office

Mahoney MR (1997) The Social Construction of Whiteness in Degaldo R and Stefancic J (eds) (1997) *Critical White Studies: looking beyond the mirror* Philadelphia: Temple University Press

Metropolitan Police Service (no date) *A Police Service for all the People: developing strategies to attract, retain and develop ethnic minority recruits in the Metropolitan Police Service and to prepare suitable officers for the most senior ranks* MPS

Morgan G (1985) The analysis of ethnicity: conceptual problems and policy implications *New Community* Vol 12 No 3

Murji K and Cutler D (1990) From a Force into a Service? the police, racial attacks and equal opportunities in *Critical Social Policy* Issue 29 Vol. 10 No. 2 Autumn Longman: Essex

Nakayama T and Krizek R (1999) Whiteness as Strategic Rhetoric in Nakayama T and Martin N (eds) *Whiteness: the Communication of Social Identity* London: Sage

National Strategy for Neighbourhood Renewal (2000) *Report of Policy Action Team 12: Young People* March London: Stationery Office

Nkomo SM (1992) The Emperor has No Clothes: rewriting 'Race in Organisations' in *Academy of Management Review* vol. 17 no. 3 487- 513

Norton Taylor R (1999) *The Colour Of Justice: the Stephen Lawrence Inquiry* London: Oberon Books

Nottinghamshire Police Audit (1999) *Internal Audit of Police and Community/Race Relations: In response to HMIC Report 'Winning the Race – Policing Plural Communities* Nottingham:NPA

OFSTED Report (1999) *Raising the Attainment of Ethnic Minority Pupils* London: OFSTED

Osler A (1999) Citizenship, Democracy and Political Literacy in *MCT Multicultural Teaching* Vol 18 No 1

Parekh B and Hepple B (April 1999) *Seminar on Common Values* London: Commission on the Future of Multi-Ethnic Britain

Phoenix A (1988) Narrow Definitions of Culture: the case of early motherhood, in Westwood S and Bhachu P (eds.) *Enterprising Women, Ethnicity, Economy and Gender Relations* London and New York: Routledge

Phoenix (1997) 'I'm white! So what?' the construction of Whiteness for young Londoners in Fine M *et al* (eds) (1997) *Off White: readings on race, power and society* London: Routledge

Phoenix A (1998) Dealing with Difference: the recursive and the new, in *Ethnic and Racial Studies* vol. 21 no. 5

Popple K (1997) Understanding and tackling racism among young people in the United Kingdom in Laurens Hazekamp J and Popple K (eds) (1997) *Racism in Europe: a challenge for youth policy and youth work* London: UCL

Rattansi A (1994) Western Racisms Ethnicities, Identities in Rattansi A and Westwood S (eds.) *Racism Modernity and Identity on the Western Front* Cambridge: Polity

Rattansi A (1999) Racism 'Postmodernism' and Reflexive Multiculturalism in May S (ed.) *Critical Multiculturalism: rethinking multicultural and anti-racist education* Philadelphia: Falmer Press

Richardson R (1999) Unequivocal Acceptance – lessons from the Stephen Lawrence Inquiry for education *MCT Multicultural Teaching* Vol 17, No2

Rolt S 'Taking on Rural Racism: Fusion, a Devon peer education project delivers anti racism project in rural areas' *UK Youth* Autumn 1999

ROTA Briefing no.10 August 1999 *Education Under New Labour* London: ROTA

Runnymede Bulletin (1999) *Refugees: Rights and Resources no 320*

Ruunymede Trust (1997) *Islamophobia: a challenge for us all.* London: Runnymede

Runnymede Trust (1999) *Examining School Exclusions and the Race Factor* Briefing Paper December London

Runnymede Trust (2000) *The Parekh Report: Commission on the Future of Multi Ethnic Britain* Profile Books: London

Saghal G and Yuval-Davis N (eds) (1992) *Refusing Holy Orders: Women and Fundamentalism in Britain* London: Virago

Sewell T (1997) *Black Masculinities and Schooling: How Black Boys Survive Modern Schooling* Stoke On Trent: Trentham Books

Sivanandan A (1981) From Resistance to Rebellion: Asian and Afro-Caribbean Struggles in Britain in *Rebellion and Repression Race and Class* Volume XXIII, No 2/3 Autumn 1981/Winter 1982 London:IRR

Sivanandan A (1985) RAT and the degradation of the black struggle in *Race and Class* vol. 26 pp 1-33

Smaje C (1995) *Health, Race and Ethnicity: Making Sense of the Evidence* London: Kings Fund Institute

Social Exclusion and Policy Unit (2000) Action Team no.12: *Young People* March London: Stationery Office

Social Exclusion Unit (1999) *Bridging the Gap: New Opportunities for 16-18 year olds not in Education, Employment or Training* London: Stationery Office

Social Exclusion Unit (7 July 1998) *Summary of the Social Exclusion Unit's Report on Rough Sleepers* London: Social Exclusion Unit

Solomos J and Back L (1996) *Racism and Society* Basingstoke: Macmillan

Solomos J and Wrench J (1993) The Politics and Processes of Racial Discrimination in Britain in Solomos J and Wrench J (eds) *Racism and Migration in Western Europe* Oxford: Berg

Spencer S (1999) *The Need for a Human Rights Commission in Britain and its relationship with the Commission for Racial Equality: the position of the MEB* London: Institute for Public Policy Research

Spencer S (2000) *Building a Human Rights Culture* in Commission on the Future of Multiethnic Britain London: Runnymede Trust

Stephen Lawrence Inquiry (1999) *Appendices* London: Stationery Office

Swindon Racial Equality Council (1998) *Visible Women, Conference Report* SREC

Tomlinson S (2000) *Education* – Paper prepared for the Commission on the Future of Multiethnic Britain London: Runnymede Trust

Troyna B and Ball W (1985) *Views from the Chalk Face: school responses to an Lea's policy on multicultural education* Warwick: Centre for Research in Ethnic Relations

Troyna B and Williams J (1986) *Racism, Education and the State* London: Croom Helm

van Dijk TA (1993) Denying Racism: Elite Discourse and Racism in Solomos J and Wrench J (eds) *Racism and Migration in Western Europe* Oxford: Berg

van Dijk, TA (1999) *Discourse and Racism in Discourse and Society* Volume 10 (2) April

Wander P, Martin N and Nakayama T (1999) Whiteness and Beyond in Nakayama T and Martin N (eds) *Whiteness: the communication of social identity* London: Sage

Ware V (1997) Island Racism: Gender, Place and White Power, in Frankenberg R *Displacing Whiteness* Durham: Duke University Press

West Midlands County Council (1986) *A Different Reality: an account of black people's experiences and their grievances before and after the Handsworth Rebellions of September 1985* Report of the Review Panel: West Midlands CC: Birmingham

Wieivorka M (1995) *The Arena of Racism* London: Sage

Willems H (1995) Right Wing Extremism, Racism or Youth Violence? Explaining Violence Against Foreigners in Germany in *New Community* 21(4) 1995 pp501-523

Williams R (1976) *Keywords* London: Fontana.

Wimmer A 'Explaining Xenophobia and Racism' in *Ethnic and Racial Studies* volume 20 (1) 1997

Woodward K (1997) *Identity and Difference* London: Sage Open University Press

Yuval- Davis N (1997) *Gender and Nation* London and Thousand Oaks,New Delhi: Sage

Newspaper articles referred to

The Independent 29 May 1997 'Straw to abandon Tory asylum laws'

The Independent 17 June 1997 'Tighter rules to deport illegal asylum seekers'

The Guardian 28 June 1997 'You may be alright Jack, but people are suffering out there'

The Guardian 22 August 1997 'Minister plans review of asylum'

The Times 20 October 1997 'Dover overwhelmed by Gypsy asylum-seekers'

The Independent 23 October 1997 'Immigration chiefs fear influx of more gypsy 'refugees'

The Observer 26 October 1997 'No gypsies please, we're British: In Dover, human kindness flows thinly'

The Independent 26 October 1997 ''They steal – not that I've met any myself': Gypsy asylum seekers in Dover face wall of prejudice'

The Independent 28 October 1997 'Asylum seekers reach a record high'

The Times 28 October 1997 'Appeal time is cut for bogus refugees'

The Independent 28 October 1997 'New curb on bogus asylum seekers'

The Independent 15 November 1997 'Dover braces itself for NF march on asylum hostel: the National Front will today be allowed to March in Dover to stir up emotions over the recent arrival of Romany asylum seekers'

The Independent 16 November 1997 'Two hurt as racists march in Dover'

The Independent 16 November 1997 'Gypsies flee from violence'

The Independent 29 November 1997 'Synod backs rethink on immigration: we need to rethink our policy on asylum seekers'

The Guardian 17 February 1999 'Asylum: cruel myths'

The Guardian 23 February 1999 'Straw widens immigration checks on UK entrants'

The Guardian 10 March 1999 'Bad neighbours'

The Observer 2 May 1999 'Straw backs down over asylum laws'

The Guardian 5 May 1999 'Halt the asylum bill'

The Observer 9 May 1999 'Asylum law uproar: refugee policy at cross purposes'

The Times 11 May 1999 'An act that shames us all'

The Guardian 13 May 1999 'Comment and analysis: Asylum abusers'

The Guardian 4 June 1999 'Seeking asylum'

The Guardian 9 June 1999 'Straw moves to quell asylum bill rebellion'

The Observer 22 August 1999 'Plight of asylum seekers: from here, Dover looks good'

The Guardian 30 August 1999 ' Hague keeps up pressure on asylum'

The Guardian 8 October 1999 'Plan for dispersal of asylum seekers'

The Times 8 October 1999 'Britain to soak up thousands seeking asylum'

The Guardian 21 October 1999 'Vouchers defeat for Straw holds up asylum bill'

The Guardian 9 November 1999 'Improving asylum'

The Observer 5 December 1999 'Without prejudice: put them in a ghetto and chuck away the key'

The Guardian 21 February 2000 'Race: a special report one year after Macpherson'

The Guardian 22 March 2000 'The Sun's gypsy curse'

The Guardian 27 March 2000 'The asylum debate: on the long road to Britain'

The Guardian 27 March 2000 'Riot at funeral of police victim'

The Guardian 28 March 2000 'Dover, no port in a storm for refugees'

The Guardian 28 March 2000 'What is Britishness? Tories dream while Labour defines'

The Guardian 28 March 2000 'Labour tries to reclaim the flag: ministers launch debate on modern Britishness to resolves party's problem and put pressure on Hague'

The Guardian 1 April 2000 'Bridging Britain's Social divide: neighbourhood renewal'

The Guardian 10 April 2000 'Labour and Tories reported for inflammatory asylum language'

The Guardian 11 April 2000 'Clampdown inflames asylum row: Kent ban could be followed by 20 councils'

The Guardian 2 May 2000 'Racists are so blind': immigrant workers make us richer not poorer'.

The Guardian 8 May 2000 'Neo-Nazis send death threat to Ali-G'

The Guardian 8 May 2000 'Profile of Mayor's race advisors'

The Guardian 8 May 2000 'Unbridled ride to rights: devolution has brought a year of surprises for the Scottish legal system. From October, England too has shocks in store'

The Guardian 8 May 2000 'We're growing too old. We need more immigrants'

The Guardian 16 May 2000 'So who gets the job?'

The Observer 2 July 2000 'Race victims await their fate: the gypsies were forgotten victims of the holocaust. Now Britain is deciding the future of Roma asylum seekers fleeing a new racism'

The Guardian 6 July 2000 'FA club faces purge of racist fans'

Appendix I

List of materials in the search at the CRE library (in date order)

Industrial training boards on race relations development in race relations training and advisory work since the discussion
Corp. Author: Commission for Racial Equality
Publisher: BACIE/ CRE
Year: 1977/ 1978
CRE Class: nd31

White Awareness: handbook for anti racism training
Author: Katz J
Publisher: University of Oklahoma,
Year: Feb 1979
CRE Class: DD62

Police Probationer training in race relations
Author: Southgate P
Publisher: Home Office
Year: 1982
CRE Class: le21

Community and race relations training for the police report of the Police report of the Police Training Council working party
Author: Police Training Council
Corp. Author: Home Office
Publisher: London Home Office
Year: 1983
CRE Class: le6

The Fourth R: race issues in police training
Author: Howells R
Corp. Author: Glare (Greater London Action for Racial Equality)
Publisher: Glare
Year: 1983
CRE Class: le35

Industrial language training: A study and experiment in race awareness training for metropolitan police probationers
Author: Christmas E
Corp. Author: National Centre for Industrial Language Training
Publisher: Industrial Language Training 1983
Year: 1983
CRE Class: le26

HMP Pentonville race relations and training package designed for local staff training based on 1976 race relations act
Author: Covington C
Corp. Author: HMP Prison
Publisher: HMP Prison
Year: 1984
CRE Class: lg38

Racism awareness training for the police report of a pilot study by the Home Office
Author: Southgate P
Corp. Author: Home Office
Publisher: London Home Office
Year: 1984
CRE Class: le29

RAT and the degradation of black struggle
Author: Sivanandan, A
Publisher: Race and Class 1985
Year: 1985
CRE Class: dc164

Racism Awareness Training
Corp. Author: Race Equality Policy Group
Publisher: London Strategic Policy Unit
Year: 1987
CRE Class: DC100

Racism what's it got to do with me?
Corp. Author: British Youth Council
Publisher: BYC
Year: 1987
CRE Class: dc187

Staff Development for a multi-cultural society: strategies for mainly white areas
Corp. Author: Further Education Unit
Publisher: Further Education Unit
Year: 1988
CRE Class: ke57

Racial equality and the prison service
Corp. Author: Commission for Racial Equality
Publisher: Commission for Racial Equality
Year: 1989
CRE Class: Ig23

Training for Racial Equality in Housing – a guide
Corp. Author: Commission for Racial Equality
Publisher: CRE
Year: 1989
CRE Class: if73

Communities of resistance – writings on black struggles for socialism
Author: Sivanandan, A
Publisher: Verso
Year: 1990
CRE Class: DC128

Policing and race equality in the Netherlands: positive action initiatives in recruitment and training
Author: Oakley R
Corp. Author: Police Foundation
Publisher: Police Foundation
Year: 1990
CRE Class: Ie36

Racism awareness training: a radio discussion
Author: Baksk, Q and Oakley R
Corp. Author: London Borough of Waltham Forest
Publisher: London Borough of Waltham Forest
Year: 1990
CRE Class: nd121

Combating racism through training: a review of approaches to race training in organisations (policy paper in ethnic relations no 22)
Corp. Author: Centre for Research in Ethnic Relations/University of
                 Warwick
Publisher: Centre for Research in Ethnic Relations
Year: 1991
CRE Class: dc251

Training for equality: a study of race relations and equal opportunities training
Author: Lawton J and Brown C
Corp. Author: Policy Studies Institute
Publisher: London Policy Studies Institute
Year: 1991
CRE Class: NF51

Training implementing racial equality at work
Corp. Author: Commission for Racial Equality
Publisher: CRE
Year: 1991
CRE Class: nd39

Police access training a case study of positive action and ethnic minority
recruitment to the West Midlands police force
Author: Tolley H and Thomas K
Corp. Author: Commission for Racial Equality
Publisher: Commission for Racial Equality
Year: 1992
CRE Class: le38

Improving practice in the criminal justice system
Author: De Gale H, Hanlon P, Hubbard M and Morgan S
Corp. Author: Central Council for Education and Training in Social Work
Publisher: CCETSW
Year: 1993
CRE Class: lf80

Improving practice teaching and learning
Author: Humphries B, Pankhama-Wimmer H, Seale A and Stoke I
Corp. Author: Central Council for Education and Training in Social Work
                 (CCETSW)
Publisher: CCETSW
Year: 1993
CRE Class: JM56

Race and criminal justice: training: a report of the NACRO race issues advisory
committee
Corp. Author: Nacro Race Issue Advisory Committee
Publisher: NACRO
Year: 1993
CRE Class: lf132

The Chinese in Tameside taking the initiative assessing the needs of improving
practice
Author: Phillpot G, O'Neil A and Lee K
Publisher: Tameside Metropolitan Borough 1994
Year: 1994
CRE Class: eb22

Unloading the Cultural Baggage
Author: Crawford L
Publisher: New Impact
Year: June July 1994

Teaching race and ethnicity: disciplinary perspectives
Author: Bulmer M and Solomos J
Publisher: *Ethnic and racial studies*
Year: October 1996

Tell it like it is
Author: Bond H
Publisher: *Community Care*
Year: 2-8 May 1996
CRE Class: microfiche

Themes and issues in the teaching of race and ethnicity in sociology
Author: Mason D
Publisher: *Ethnic and racial studies*
Year: October 1996

Improving uptake of breast screening in multi-ethnic populations: a randomised
controlled trial using practice reception staff to contact non-attenders
Author: Atri J, Gregg R, Robson J, Omar RZ and Dixon S
Publisher: *British Medical Journal*
Year: 1997

Reading social work: competing discourses in the rules and requirements for the
Diploma in social work
Author: Humphries B
Publisher: *British Journal of Social Work*
Year: 1997
CRE Class: ja114

Education and racism: a cross-national survey of positive effects of education on
ethnic tolerance
Author: Hagendoorn L and Nekuee S
Publisher: Ashgate
Year: 1999
CRE Class: pc127

House of Commons: session 1998-1999: Home Affairs Committee:
1) Police training and recruitment;
2) delays in the immigration and nationality directorate;
3) accountability of the security service: minutes of evidence Tuesday 20 April 1999
Author: Straw, Rt Hon Jack MP, Pugh P and Woodward A
Corp. Author: House of Commons
Publisher: HMSO
Year: 1999
CRE Class: le140

A report on the seminar on racism awareness training
Corp. Author: Commission for Racial Equality
Publisher: CRE
CRE Class: dc162
Date   31 October 1984

Improving mental health practice: a training manual
Author: Clarke P, Harrison M and Patel K
Publisher: Leeds Northern Curriculum Development Project
Date: November 1992
CRE Class: JL204

Improving practice with elders: a training manual
Author: Ahmad A A, Richardson I, Whittaker T and Leung T
Corp. Author: Central Council for Education and Training in Social Work
                 (CCETSW)
Publisher: CCETSW Leeds
Date: 1992
CRE Class: jp53

Race and social policy unit: a research training and advisors services
Author: Liverpool University
Corp. Author: Commission for Racial Equality
Publisher: Commission for Racial Equality
CRE Class: j15
Undated

Racism Awareness training
Author: Ohri A
Date: 1985
CRE Class: dc170

Towards effective race relations training
Author: Peppard N
Publisher: New Community
Date: 1980 Vol VIII spring/Summer
CRE Class: dc104

Appendix II

This analysis by Stella Dadzie clearly indentifies the strengths and weaknesses of the various aproaches that have been adopted to try to tackle racism. Dadzie shows that there are significant pitfalls in every approach.

(from *Tookit for Tackling Racism in Schools* by Stella Dadzie, 2000 p.69-71, published by Trentham Books)

APPROACHES TO TACKLING RACISM

Approaches	Advantages	Drawbacks	Delivered Via..	Requires
INFORMATIVE: teaching the facts about racial disadvantage, slavery, immigration etc.	Provides an historical and political basis for understanding and debating complex issues	Assumes racism results from irrationality or ignorance May underestimate the strength of institutional and ideological racism May alienate young people if too school like	Structured or formal learning contexts Tasks/guest speakers Films/videos Theatre workshops Input into the community e.g. local antiracist campaigns	Access to relevant resources and time to research/develop them Appropriate room and atmosphere for formal learning activity Identified fund for speakers , books, posters, video hire etc Staff/external expertise
MULTICULTURAL: Organising cultural activities, event, exchanges to increase understanding of other cultures	Encourages contact and appreciation of the benefits of cultural diversity Provides an opportunity to 'sample' or experience aspects of the other culture May increase understanding	Defines 'cultural differences' as the problem May assume the dominant culture is the norm into which others would integrate Encourages a 'zoo' mentality by emphasising the exotic or curious May reinforce existing prejudices Overlooks questions of power and hierarchy-both central to racism	Visits/exchanges/travel attending festivals Events or in-house activities involving cookery, music, dance traditional dress etc. Parental/community involvement Input into the community e.g. voluntary work	Adequate finances to resource outings/activities/events Active contact with parents and community groups Some staff awareness of relevant issues of cultural diversity

APPROACHES TO TACKLING RACISM

Approaches	Advantages	Drawbacks	Delivered Via..	Requires
EXPERIENTIAL: encouraging identification with what it's like to be a victim	Encourages personal identification with what it feels like to be excluded, harassed, ridiculed, etc Heightens awareness of the effect sof racist behaviour	Relies on its emotional appeal Trivialises racism by defining it as isolated acts of individual or local injustice	Formal/informal workshops Involving discussions and/or role play Organised games/activities	Appropriate rooms for games and workshop activities Staff able to handle group dynamics
MORALISTIC: appealing to a common sense of decency	Provides a 'moral yardstick' with which to challenge racism; May have a positive influence on attitudes/behaviour in other areas	May be effective in the short term but leaves historic and political roots of racism unchallenged	Drawing attention to personal/ social injustices; Formal/ informal religious or moral instruction; Input into the community via for example fund raising activities Involvement in humanitarian campaigns	Liaison with religious/ humanitarian organisations Morally persuasive staff
ATTITUDINAL: providing counselling or racism awareness training	Encourages greater self awareness	Too personalised or psychologically orientated, resulting in individual 'guilt tripping' or defensiveness Emphasises personal responsibility rather than collective responses May ignore issues of institutional power	Structured discussion with groups/individuals Residential/non residential training sessions Selected group activities Role play theatre workshops etc.	In house expertise or input form an outside trainer Staff knowledge of basic counselling skills

APPROACHES TO TACKLING RACISM

Approaches	Advantages	Drawbacks	Delivered Via...	Requires
PUNTIVE: automatic punishment of racist members ANTAGONISTIC: responding to hard core racists in a language they can understand	Gives everyone a clear message that racism will not be tolerated Counteracts feelings of helplessness in the target or victim	Results in the punishment or banning of overtly racist individuals rather than an enlightened group response Relies on sanctions or force resulting in alienation or polarised loyalties Suppresses overt racist activity but fails to challenge the ideology behind it	Direct and if necessary verbal or physical confrontation Adherence to an enforceable antiracist code of conduct Realistic sanctions	Public Code of Conduct Clear enforceable sanctions Assertive staff
BLACK ONLY PROVISION: offering self/cultural//historical awareness –raising for identifies groups of black young people	provides a 'safe' forum for exploring shared experience of blackness, racism, exclusion, displacement, etc promotes assertiveness and positive feelings of cultural/social identity	May assume one shared experience and overlook important religious/cultural/ linguistic diversities Encourages assumptions about preferential treatment among those excluded thus risking further isolation/harassment of targeted group	Formal/informal group discussions Use of talks/videos/plays/ exhibitions to examine relevant social and cultural issues Music/cookery/other cultural activities ESOL/community language provision	Community consultation and outreach Community input Access to adequate/ relevant resources Staff with sufficient consciousness/expertise